ALSO BY CHARLES NORTH

POETRY
Lineups
Elizabethan & Nova Scotian Music
Six Buildings
Leap Year: Poems 1968-1978
The Year of the Olive Oil
New & Selected Poems
The Nearness of the Way You Look Tonight
Cadenza
Complete Lineups

PROSE
No Other Way: Selected Prose
Ode to Asparagus, Peonies and Manet

COLLABORATIONS
Gemini (with Tony Towle)
Tulips (with Trevor Winkfield)

EDITOR
Broadway: A Poets and Painters Anthology (with James Schuyler)
Broadway 2: A Poets and Painters Anthology (with James
    Schuyler)

WHAT IT
IS LIKE

WHAT IT IS LIKE

NEW AND SELECTED POEMS

CHARLES NORTH

Turtle Point Press / Hanging Loose Press

Printed in the United States of America
10 9 8 7 6 5 4 3 2 1

Hanging Loose Press, 231 Wyckoff Street, Brooklyn, NY 11217.
www.hangingloosepress.com.

Hanging Loose Press thanks the Literature Program of the New York
State Council on the arts for a grant in support of the publication of
this book.

Turtle Point Press, www.turtlepointpress.com

Many of these poems originally appeared in the following collections:
Elizabethan & Nova Scotian Music (Adventures in Poetry, 1974); *Six
Buildings* (Swollen Magpie, 1977); *Leap Year: Poems 1968–1978* (Kulchur,
1978); *The Year of the Olive Oil* (Hanging Loose, 1989); *New and Selected
Poems* (Sun & Moon, 1999); *The Nearness of the Way You Look Tonight*
(Adventures in Poetry, 2001); and *Cadenza* (Hanging Loose, 2007).

Poems in the "New Poems" section were published, in whole or in part,
in *Angle, Aphros, The Brooklyn Rail, Gerry Mulligan, Hanging Loose, The
Hat, Maggy, Pataphysics, The Poker, Poetry Poject Newsletter, Portable Boog
Reader, Sal Mimeo, Shiny, The Sienese Shredder, Tight, Vanitas,* and *Zoland
Poetry.* The author thanks the editors and regrets any omissions.

Library of Congress Cataloging-in-Publication Data available on request.
ISBN: 978-1-933527-48-2

CONTENTS

NEW POEMS

for Paula

and in memory of Paul Violi

ELIZABETHAN &

NOVA SCOTIAN MUSIC

1974

POEM

Now that I am seeing myself as a totally different person
whose interests are like a street covered with slush
and whose every word rings like the car of a spaniel

night joins with its various egos, its tubeless containers
of islands being joined by the notion of paradise
and I am swept up in what it means to be drained, or

a little less like those pastels that hung around
sopping up every loose glove of moisture where the bay
wasn't defined by its shoreline. Yet that air and that sun

did us both good and the thieving blue jays were enjoyable
as dots on boards, beside rabbits, sparrows, and herrings
numerous trails each of which wound into the other's thicket

where it got new earths and new strengths, and flashed on the
screen, sparkling like corn as the sun went down each dusk.

To the Book

Open poetry died with Whitman.
Closed poetry died with Yeats.
Natural poetry was born and died with Lorca
And Clare, also with France's Jean de Meung.
The feeling of being caught (and held)
Is reproduced in the sonneteers of the English Renaissance,
With the exception of one very great poet whose work opens.
Cars, lights, and love belong to Catullus
And to the Chinese, and to the death of symbolism
In Henry Vaughan, naturalism's decay
In Stephen Crane, the growth and moribundity
Of obsessive sex à la the works of Ponge and MacPherson
And in Basho, Li Po, and Fitzgerald (and Khayam).
Mannerism in Emerson, consumption in Leopardi,
Sleep and poetry in Sappho, Nash, Swift,
Gibran and Coleridge; decadence,
Humor, Platonism, hysteria, line endings, skald,
And the quality of unearthly, though unhysterical, beauty
In John Skelton and Anne Bradstreet; François
De Malherbe and Vosnesensky, what qualities are dead
In you that will have their rebirth here?

ELIZABETHAN & NOVA SCOTIAN MUSIC

What will see us through, a certain calm
Born of the willingness to be not cowed
The begonia idea of the universe
And because life is so short
A way of being unfaithful like the tide
Minus its characteristic awareness.

Moving is the world and all its creatures
Known by the things that surround it
Love, money, titles, the periphrastic way
Of being other than we are not
Throughout the long afternoon of language
Attractive though dead, such calm falling

And issuing in a well-meant spiel
Involving money as a metaphor: Money is
The only metaphor and because life is short
A gross keyboard of light and sometimes strength
As well to be aware of its fickleness
As stab it in the back with gentleness.

POEM

When you consider how Europe flashes by
like a vowel, and in obsolete whispers
or in uttering in a whisper, talking or saying
privately or secretly and having a curved
outside or form especially like the Joan of Arc
of a flame, or characterized by full spontaneous
movement not in a circle, not cramped or limited
but free & vigorous in motion as an integer—
then anything within the sphere of a number
globe or ring, a group such as positions
or any course ending where it began, is as
complete as you are, and ends where you began,
loosely or simultaneously reprieved (like air)
or the space below, which is perfect, less rare

MADRIGAL: ANOTHER LIFE

I like very much the notion that I will
Appear in another life. I like
The notion of another life with its cares
Its concerts, its flamboyances
Its caresses, its nouns and its words
Which will take the place of nouns.

Villa Capra's Sestina

Across "the sensuality of shade" shadows move in parenthetical
    truisms.
If color seems to be the reflection in its most vivid form
Of the world already past, there is great variety in the way we
    take its effects
The journalism of deepest and most enduring feelings.
The fact that an artist has created the illusion of depth
And that it is significant of the way we understand depth

Creates a limitless depth. (The attention shifts reproducingly.)
Of the past thirty centuries: whether from above or below
Or near or far its original may be useful but is in no sense a garden
Built up from a unique sample. A good
Example is the necessity of influencing the past
By the journalism of deepest and most enduring feelings

The present, the past and the future, the relations of the arts
To food, hunger and sex, prints, knotty clouds (as organized in
    Perugino)
To combine what is otherwise a soft blending of those totally
Other values resonance, shadow and conception. To achieve peace
Demands peacefulness, forget those totally other values.
A timeless introduction! Where a transition engulfs extremes

All contrasts glowingly with the history of limitless depth
Dominating the relationship of the arts to food, hunger and sex,
The so called habiliments of our wit. "I am a melancholy struggle
With gymnastics." Plodding warmth echoes and to escape
    whether from above or below
Requires a Mnemosyne beyond nature's although it does not
    seem
To relate to specific pasts and seems to originate in a real

Interest in describing what is immediately before us
The opposite is hunger, food and sex, the distribution of wealth
And we are bearers of fog like the Villa Capra. There is an
    impression
Of notes flapping to be restored, the glowingly different
    appearance
In training ushering in a journalism of the deepest and most
    enduring feelings
And whether from above or below (or near or far) the example

Of the arts, a garden built up from a unique sample, though to
    achieve peace
A monumental peacefulness overlooked on first view but
    hammered
As opposed to the nicety of the regular schedule of our feelings
Which, like the past thirty centuries, reproduced
Depends on this polished vagueness
The fact that an artist has created the illusion of depth.

SOME VERSIONS OF REEDS
for Kenneth Koch

If the box is tightly sealed, break it open.
(That is, tear through the gold opaque Scotch tape.)
Twenty-five shafts of varying color—
Though all exist in a well-defined area
Somewhere between straw and wheat (cf. bamboo)
And shaped like wedges, approximately two
And one-half inches long and about two-fifths
Of an inch wide, flat on the underside
And gently rounded over the top for half
The length, whereas the playing portion (a term
Usually reserved for between the foul lines)
Curves much more subtly and flattens at the tip
Where the cane has been shaved and progressively
Narrows like a woman's leg, but unlike
A woman progressively translucent, with the tip
Echoing the topographical curve
Like neap tide on a beach; twenty-five pieces
Of cane, undistinguished except for the name,
Dutch, but looking for all the world like French
With the words *marque déposée* and *supérieure*
Indicating that in some French-speaking
Country the name was registered like wine,
And that among the echelons of reeds

There are none higher—but looking once again
"Made in France" is clearly written on the bottom
Of the lavender cover, so the French-speaking country
Is France, and the person or family who gave
Their name to the superior reeds is as misleading
As Kees Van Dongen; still you can't help being
Aware that "superior" doesn't have the ring
Of *supérieure*—in fact a loss of music
Such as seems apparent to some in viewing
All modern art, but which is more clearly seen
As a retranslation of music, keeping all
The best that word implies while throwing out
The tired or used portion which in time can make
People shudder at "modern-what?" and finally
Close their eyes and ears. And so the preceding
Fragment, even though its meaning hasn't
Been gathered into the coral living room
Of the sentence, has its meaning even so,
Another characteristic of modern art.
If you pick one up and hold it to the light
You will immediately see the difference
Between the base or shaft and the coarser part
Which touches the player's lips, a paradox
(Or seeming contradiction) which is clear
Later. The shaft is shiny, often colored
Irregularly, with brownish dots and blotches
And sometimes cracks like knots in pine paneling;

Though sometimes absolutely pure, the cane
Reflecting daylight like the shiny surface
Of a lake which one is too far from to see
Oneself in and has to go closer, drawn
By the beauty of the sky overhead, the smells
Of woods and flowers and the person alongside.
They look a little like a skin disease
But more like logs (they are cane, after all)
Planed by the incessant motion of
Rushing water and smoothed, like whitecaps, by
The loggers' feet, which like surfers' must have
An intelligence of their own to avoid the ultimate
Pratfall of depth. But this isn't about logs.
The life of a reed exists in a format drawn
To squeeze the most energy out of it,
Which in music translates as sound, more precisely
Vibration which pushes the sound outwards
Through charged air to engage the audience
In a Socratic dialogue of beauty:
Who first prepared, then stranded, are moved
Silently upward to exist on a plane
Different from their own yet at the same time
What they could be, pure potentiality,
The distinction from which is as close as that
Between Donne's air and angels, so that it
Isn't really there. But to insure all this,
To prevent the noisy occupational hazard

Players call squeaks, takes all the player has,
Beginning with choosing the best available reeds,
And winding up on the stage alone—but including
Also the inventory of techniques
To improve a reed and pull from it even more
Than it originally had. Clipping the tip
Shifts the energy of the reed forward;
Shaving or sanding it with a razor blade,
Sandpaper or Dutch rush (again the Dutch!)
Makes a hard reed "speak." But of course if after
Clipping and sanding the player's initial attack
Is a moment late, or blurred like vision during
A migraine or a whirlwind love affair
Or a quiet dream in which only good things
Were permitted to speak, and then in a whisper
(But audible enough to make the morning sweet)
Then is the time to reject a reed outright.
To store the best reeds, those chosen and worked
—Besides clipping and sanding, some players
Knead the surface with plain paper to knit
The fibers; others give new reeds a bath
In tap water to prevent "water-logging"
Later on when it counts; I once knew someone
Who stored reeds in black tea—and tested through
The gamut of notes from the lowest F
To high C (passing through the *chalumeau*
Renowned for its dark wood and deep contours,

While above, the sound is cold and clear like a day
In Maine), place them on a flat square of glass
And loop a rubber band around them, say,
Two on each side; you can buy a metal clip
Which serves the same purpose, but it's a gyp
At $4.00. And so having done all
That is humanly possible, short of human error
—Which is copilot in so many airplane crashes—
The rest depends on finding a mentor who
Will draw you out of yourself (assuming there
Is something there, which doesn't fade or fray
In light), studying, and having what there
Isn't a name for, soul or character
Or whatever divides the masters from the rest
Who occupy the orchestra desks—not
That they are bad musicians but that in music
As in most things there is a point where talent
Falls down and the ambulance with silver
Tires and a blue flag resembling the sea,
Or genius, must hurry to pick it up, lest talent
Be seen for what it is, sometimes unhappily
So. Technique is a matter of practice,
Character a matter of fate, and encouragement
The work of the Times—not the newspaper—
But tone can be an indicator of genius
And it depends on muscle as much as breath.
For just as a coal miner's headlight clamped

To his head keeps him from cracking it open
On jutting rocks, the proper control of lips,
Diaphragm and stomach keeps the tone
Whole as it emerges from the bell
To expand in the air of the concert hall;
For the real beauty of tone may not be
Apparent to those close by, needing the space
Between the stage and audience to grow.
The richest tone may sound nasally thin
Up close, but further the thinness turns to strength
And like a natural gas pipe rising from
The deepest parts of the earth, expands until
It resembles nothing so much as outer life,
The mixture of gases (and sound) in which we live.
But in order to produce the expanding flow
Of sound, the reed first and foremost must be
As flawless as gold—less often, the golden
Reed with flaws may be compensated for
By a player's subtle changes in embouchure
(Which interestingly also means "expansion
Of a river valley into a plain," suggesting
That mouth and mouth of a river are similar
Enough to stand for one another in
A dream, kissing the mouth of Nauset Bay
And waking with your smell infusing the air
Like the richest tea, whose color like whiskey
And amber colors every notion of

The natural life) or pressure: by tightening
His lips and muscles and breathing properly
From the diaphragm, as in love one compensates
For weakness with emotion, overcoming
Obstacles—"sound" here being inspired
Stretches amid deserts of obscurity
Hence most inspiring to those who learn its flow,
Via the mysterious physiology
That makes us stop and listen attentively
To its rushes and sometimes exceed ourselves.

Japanese Woman Beside The Water

As rain is bending the urgent pine needles
which are pointing towards the sun
shooting past the tin and worn wood bird houses
and the earth-colored feeder tray on which two sticks have
    reversed
while the roof no barrier smokes in its rays
and they make a noise like cars plowing through surf
like warmed frozen pizza so it is an outdoors
of cheese melting and dripping down frozen window panes
where new rivulets of seeds of tomato vines
have almost come back to life in the ravishing gloom of late sky
under the burden of August just visible as
jets of vapor past the swamp in a compact to drink
dope before going to bed or else cement them to the ground
in a composition of brown grass and silver nitrate
enveloping the bay in its tough arms
angry almost eye color the extremely hot asphalt
almost lightning though it is lightening as the church
this morning so blue as here hundreds of miles away
practically speaking a totally different country
but rain seems just as wet as if you left a piece of bread out
on a plate overnight the yeast of the sky and its hips
and later we live for the sky in her arms

A Few Facts About Me

I am moved often, and easily
without knowing why or finding it appropriate
to be a consequence of somebody else's unfathomable will.

I can be taken in by the suggestion of emotion in others
even if their actions are as foreign to human psychology
as the emotions of European children in American textbooks

or American textbooks in American life. Deciding what my life
will be has always been the decision as to what it has been,
and before I met you I knew what it would be like, and planned
    to be in the path

of whatever could change it, whether or not it prevented me
from being the sole translator of your natural eloquence.
As the captain of my fate and steerer of my star

I don't find any single decision irrevocable,
feeling inadequate to life's daily immensities, a condition
of the unwillingness to act, for of the things that are human

the best is to be unavoidable, which doesn't make it any better
but doesn't make it worse—like that sunset I'm always refusing
    to look behind
or away from as if to be dull were the reverse of not shining

and living selfishly when that too is exhaustible.

Naming Colors

A perfect cream
                its middle reaches up
Wheaties ravishes the lower two-fifths
Geraniums thin as boxers' ears rip
The hem and catch light stars falling

And hair like a constellation of winter
Vegetables redeems the purple plain
Acorn squash, Idaho potato, philodendron,
Raw chestnut and grape ivy sweep the page

And become the pink and the lighter blue

SIX BUILDINGS

1977

MAGIC

The cars rush along creating the ocean
which in turn creates the cars.
Meanwhile the baby is up and looking at everything
with a crown of sunlight on her head
where the hair should be. Most babies
are bald at a certain age, acquire some hair
and then are bald again, though eighty percent
of the population wear wigs so you don't generally know.

A lawn mower *thuts* below down the hill,
on the way to the ocean
which is a milky blue (or else the sky is,
reflected in it) and the sky and the sea,
and the lawn mower, are reflected in the air,
filled to capacity and coming apart,
blowing sand and milk over everyone.

CHAUCER

Into that society Geoffrey Chaucer was born and he died
without seeing it return to the way he knew it, partly through
his agency. One can imagine the sight of the Peasants drawn
up outside the walls of the city, throwing fear into the hearts
of King Richard and his nobles, of which Chaucer was one
and barely escaped with his life after the reprisals that followed
hard upon the unwillingness of privilege to dispense with its
ornaments. Fortunately Sir John Fastolf, then a judge in the
courts, was a good friend of Chaucer's, or the poet might not
have lived to produce the works he did. As it was, of the 120
projected Tales, Chaucer managed to complete only a handful,
and it is on these that his reputation rests; and when the Plague
like a guided missile struck down half of London, it did so
by bypassing the city's Chief Customs Inspector. As Chaucer
escaped both the Plague and the Rebellion of the Peasants, so I
escaped not knowing you, etc. etc.

THE BROOKLYNESE CAPITAL
some kennings for Paul Violi

The Asia of New England
The parasol bath
The nose brandisher
Zito's gold
Wall cookies
The ruby throated massage parlor
The deflector of the night's June
Bowery omelets
The beret of age
The whale cartel
The milky flashlight
Glue-fingered dawn
The critic of peace
Winter's decoder
The Zabar's of Tuscany
Mortality's reiterator
Hudson River whitefish
The foot wigwam
Bees' distraction for the armpit
The second baseman of composers
Wheat tweezing
The light slurper
The weekend divider

The face's mood ring
Ambition's "Green Monster"
The smegma convention
Hod carrier of the arms
Samuel Greenbergs
The mouse that plucks the sea stallion's aimlessness
The Anglophile of languages
Wisdom's tourniquet
The gravy sopper
The meadow cantabile
Tennis victims
Sewer corps de ballet
The Netherlands of lips
The mouth flounder
The parasitic trade
Pam & Jerrys
The pill pushing race
The fisher for midnight oil's Cupid
The cigarette pyromaniac
The mosquito beach
Sunset's hamburger extender
The Brooklynese capital
The Gatling gun of despair
The tongue motel
Il miglior fabbro
Sexual liquid lunch
The game delayer

The rose coup

The escape from sleep

Librium gesso

The shrub settee

The rumrunner's Louisville Slugger

The penis cove

Bookcase stuffing

The deflator of leisure

The barber's friend

The fried egg ditch

The winter mannerist

The cough drop rest home

The Hal Newhouser city

The George Washington Carver of boredom

The schnitzel of the Alps

The smell way

FROM THE FRENCH

The color of coral and of your lips
Tilts the car of night and its silent axles.
The door is fragrant, the alcove large and dark.
And there among the flowers, in the dark,
I find for your fabulous hair a silent bed.

I will show you, meanwhile, the countries of snow
Where the amorous star devours and dazzles.
And where a false calm aspires to defraud
You of your gifts, the night will deafen it
In notes of your extravagant praise.

Yet to be with you while wanting you in the night
I allow you some space in which to move.
If you should appear as a blue flower
On the drape of the moon the sky will receive you,
Permitting space and voice to go without reference.

Eye Reflecting the Gold of Fall

Silver is the ruby's faded glare
Awkward silence taking it out to sea
And you away. The morning
Is its own highway, interleaded
With ears at the important points,
Each the size of a key of typewriter type.
To hornets we are all electroencephalographically
Neutral. Everyone is speaking jargon, especially
The ducks which look orange in this light;—
Sunny as a fruit tree, or as a lime drawn
From the tops of the fruit trees to the telephone wire
Dividing the ocean, whose neck is the horizon.
Some words ("like 'fuck'") require objects some of the time;
    others
Are content to be themselves, suspended like a chair,
Covered in green ink. Everyone's comet
Strikes the earth, in a way.
The birds stay where they are, stretching to get the birdseed
Until they resemble the clothesline, white
With a dark shimmer. Half-cocked, except for a hay
Riding the air, the sky pushed branches against a screen
Where some T-shirts have caught, drying in powder
That will make them stiff and fragrant. As sound is released
By the head in front, the back of the neck

In back, and out and beyond the honking.
Everyone sleeps at least part of the time, the pilot
In the plane, the oceanographer in the bathysphere,
The judge on the bench, everyone else between eating and
Going to the bathroom, the window pouring
It through like the boat.
Some of the harvest words are
Also used for hunting, making them doubly unresonant,
Like an agglutinative language
Condensed to a single word, unspoken; or
The moon with no breath on it, touching your forehead in a
    complete
Absence of what meteorologists call weather
In a country on the verge of capitulating
To its smallest city. One would steer
Carefully to the south towards the lighthouse.
Slowly the lawn quiets down.
Each berry is a species of robin, all inflect night
Like the ocean's rush over a bumpy road. As the radio
Spars with air, random to the space it occupies
To the inclusion of skin. Not the argument
From design since there are no stars to push, but thin
Points of maroon beside some gold
Letters which thud, far
Out of their cosmological depth.
Then the berries leave the trees;
The birds chase them, delivered to a prior spot where each,

Like the ocean, is inflated and simplified,
Marooned no more than late afternoon mist dispensed
From an apple tree claiming to be the air outside the room,
Supporting everything in it. In the turtle's mouth.
The turtle looks up. Trees and grass, chairs and clouds,
Sit in the middle of the lawn, the snowy lawn of the air.
With a breeze the ocean stutters, in the middle of
Mumbling. But the ship is already a blur,
Each point created for the benefit of others
Which react to it as if it were poison ivy, catching the same
    spray.
A chorus steps out of the spray. Two, in fact;
Astonished at not having made themselves known before,
With brandied snow, burning eyelashes.
You are the hotel, but you are also
The vandal, as well as the house detective.
Every spray accelerates, stops, so you can watch it;
Banging like grain like the door against ice air.

Non-Verbs

Jumping, running, boating,
Standing on the shore, watching trees move;

Hurrying the kids, locking the camper,
Waiting for the ball to drop into the glove;

Joining, bathing, batting,
Covering up, loading the truck;

Farting, eating shit,
Weaving Indian rugs, listening to the Four Aces;

Gesturing, moping, electroplating,
Committing, Little Gidding, becoming a cigar;

Snowing on the azaleas, diving for treasure,
Doing the twist, getting a rope burn;

Propitiating the household gods, Gieseking,
Uncorking, signaling by semaphore

Scenes from Montale

1
A tendered silk which is not the case by anchoring

2
The walk it sometimes seems

3
Hair it is my liquid life

4
Fluoroscoped in oil, barred to speak of voltage with its salvage
window for the society of the sea

5
Invested to you remote

6
So it shows the same

7
A mouth underneath all the shady boughs

8
(And meanwhile evening shoes in the cow)

9

Fished immersion from the marked rapid then closed

10

February to spend a birch & waited

11

Accelerating and trump the brother with ice

12

Fine hard scattering: traffic from lightened cups with tags of
    clouds' aqua mist

13

Take it away and make it sleep

14

An aura of chocolate in fog

15

Visible locks contributed

16

Cracking brilliant

17

When suddenly

18
In keeping with the violet state civil and personal

19
Pruned of lateness and buzzing

20
The impulse to

21
Assisted, besides

22
For one of its spaceships is grand and the other drifting

23
To gamble on

24
Crownings and canvas stars

25
Rowing between Polish and Portuguese

26
But monitor hardly owing

27
Catching its breath (on the telephone wires)

28
The full incidentals of squaring off

29
As if the breeze were a train and each small town the moon

30
Spilling birds onto

ELEGIACAL STUDY

Fragrant in or near the spot of its advent,
a lagoon containing the pelting rain.
Flowering trees, canned food, hammocks;
facilities for the coming together
of people in a peaceful assembly, with stands
for light refreshment, diversionary and medical facilities,
small branch libraries and facilities for exercise,
beds and further conveniences for rest and leisure
(disorder fitting as a lamp its cord)
and the suspension as from the peak of an official calm
moving like a series of clouds which
by their positions reflect the dazzling seasons,
the sea and our penchant for sky
in varied plane sections as the figure studies
the echoes of a Boeing 747 tearing through it, blue violet
for personal merit and expressed like a chair or a bathtub
or a bowling alley flowering within the limits of shade
to discourse of the solitude that the self
throughout its hundred years of solitude sees itself,
in itself though narrow as a strand of hair,
and solemnly given to those ceremonies of the serious minded
such as parades, incognito of length, breadth and thickness,
and incorrectly like a medal furnishing the heroics
with the financially sound and reasonable

whereas the concrete vagrancy like the wandering
of specific sensations swings through the heat like a shade
—causing the room to swing precariously like a lampshade—
and the re-enactment merely measures air
like the transcriptions of a soft pedal, funneling
the ground into the previously requisitioned voice intelligent
    and perquisite
on the curb decorated with rainbows of contrasting
low penetration, and up forming an archway
for the coordinates air and dampness and their solution.
Three dimensions are for that majesty specified as
belonging to metal, as being poured, formed, hardened and
    cracked;
the others under the pressure of an intensified will
that, like the evening, hyphenates into the various
orders of the undoubtedly present
(though to an observer they are as sheer as rain backed
by red hills that rise into more middle substance)
all that previously thrived on it, while
the middle occupies a plateau with a view
of grey, frequently embattled, villages
including those mentioned in the myths of other conduct,
the towns like a razor blade and the rivers
within a hair's breadth of the desert overgrown
with herbs, false herbs, false hair, castles
and the somnolent men and women
vagrant as sleep within them noting

that the air surrounding is self-reflexive,
se preparer, and from this vantage point sleeps and
gives out no information.

For Dorothy Wordsworth

After an early breakfast we hoisted sail, preferring to confront the
falls in better weather. Within the space of an hour it grew black
and thundered so mightily we thought the surface of the water
would crack! We took refuge at the singing school. . . . There were
students everywhere at work and at play, some at instruments,
some at their song, the young in one another's arms like birds
in the trees, entirely unmindful of our presence. Lunch was
pleasant, we were given a choice of fish, flesh or fowl. William
had mackerel. . . . The dishwasher was the sort to pass unnoticed
in a crowd, nonetheless he caught our attention. For he had
hung his tattered coat upon a stick and sang to himself, every
so often clapping his hands and singing louder as he saw us
watching him, as if to say a man is a paltry thing unless he has
music in his soul. Over the fireplace hung an inexpensive tile
fashioned to look like gold mosaic. The fire danced, gyrated,
inexpressible; in its movement it seemed to create objects of
air, and then to retrieve them as one might replace gold jewels
in their box. As we sat by the fire I couldn't help feeling that
if I had had the control of my destiny, like a lord or a lady the
"emperor of my body," I might have remained in that sensual
atmosphere all summer long. The evening passed pleasantly
among reflections on the day, the past few days, and the days that
were to come.

LITTLE POEM IN JULY

She has to wake up sometime.
And the chicken—
It has to leave the oven
With a whirr of wings
Out into the hyacinth sunset

Where dinner is tied
To its friend and archrival the river
Filled to overflowing with dolphins
On the monstrous head
Neck and shoulders we call time.

Or it calls us that,
Since our connection
Is purely circumstantial; sliding
Off the view this late
Almost lavender mid-July evening.

LEAP YEAR

1978

FROM SONNETS FROM THE ENGLISH

Cypresse, Firre, Larix, Yew, and Trees perpetually verdant,
An ape of Agath, a Grasshopper, an Elephant of Ambre,
A Crystall Ball, three glasses, two Spoones, and six Nuts of Crystall
With Iron pins, and handsomely overwrought like the necks
Or bridges of Musicall Instruments.
The firey solution an angle, wedge, or Elbow
An ill formed horse on the reverse, Spittle Fields
Simplicity flies away remembering the early civility
They brought upon these countreys, and forgetting
The supinity of elder days, the Metropolis of Humidity
Though some had small, yet more had pointed bottoms
To eat asphodels about the Elysian meadows
They may sit in the orchestra and obscurity
Of a black color, nothing and millions of Rhapsodies.

(Thomas Browne)

Vehicle & Wavering Colour

Where do you go when you're desperate in a quiet
way? Dear Fund Raiser: I'm delighted to
announce that our next summer's production will be
on seats, in the real water. What could be more beautiful.
—*Quiet* as a night far away from here, the traffic like
rain over streets darkened, not lit, by morning.

ELEGIACAL STUDY

A new fiber eats up nightfall blanketing it
7-month stretches between one meal and another (of roses)
blackening eyes and shelling peanuts
complimentary salted ones in silver packs spelling out your name.
Floated with oranges until actually adope on the seething
ah, because the look only hands it
and distance blisters in its fragility
where a dream has had its hair scattered beyond the glass
vaguer than dusk which makes the reservoir go down half a notch.
To disprove the awkwardness encircling the day like
a frame, borrowed from the blanks which dollies and extras
are already beginning to fill: an exit ramp
printed with the first and last letters
so as to admit confusion under the man-made sign for spring.
But of the few glowing days
overloaded with traffic, in the barn
dripped from one noon to another
with only branches intervening: blinding sun
orange fall, peeling articulation, no railroads.
The breeze monopolizes everything else.
Such that though spread the air figures lightness
informed of algal trace through kings.
What if the discovery is only that
office tower covered in felt the green inevitably dropped

angling for birds reformed with e.g. valley stiffed by a bell
and skywalks linking the trapeze with the year-round
in situ first pearled, vieux tub of the fort year
produced in quantity as oak trees flush
Wings So. endless nights a kite no a Walloon.
Seats get whittled down and begin to weigh
less than the picture of the air, or a result
of the professional nearby the atom is left out
and some cool green photon hearing affected
in a pacific way, mountaineering dovetailed
the counter to click and some jays which were watchful
to a single emotion like the point of a pencil.
So like a council overcome by needless photoco-
popular voting for an 8th art, of which
the 7th is another tendency to sleep
exfoliating the leather of a wallet stuffed with dry goods
so it dumps the contents onto memory's amber prong—really
its seashore the tube part hugging twilight as if
it were a bare-breasted ship's prow minus the prow . . .
blackening all eyes present and the barely felt.
The nape officially stamp crashing fit
central wince vacant, wage and hour club vacant,
vacant merlin whose wrench came due
and downtown that dry blaze as when you smoothed
primrosed with candled looks to arms
that specifically spike its Port-Lamy to an optical rug
unread less—resolved ad seriatum among its counterparts

a fingertip through which a pencil flashlight glows
and earth's jittery frontier buckled into genetic capes
under which loosely 30 m.p.h. yellows chamfered.
Off its suffused awards revealing the trawler
covering the ceiling with eucalyptus once a week
and embed with forgetfulness an inter- & her cheek
decal mania serving the city in the meantime to adhere
elegant rifling and padded stood by to vote
forest & co. suffered solid mental reactions prediction a reality
caught like snow, an hour at a time, life-size rooms
from uptown waxing for miles southern controls
lest more nasal charms outlast if not orange nationals removed
to the view of it approximately two feet wide.
Raised to get a look at the winds
all particles sugars the morning attraction
twitched and lit peppered to scorch on soaps below

LINES

As farming and evening,
taken together, are
the same thing. The morning air

dents a jar of tulips
and interurban affairs are wasted
with the dispatch of an elegant theory.

The empowerment
of leaders begins its arduous journey
through permanent display, pink

a parade of points, green
turning out products, linking
highway to art to meta-abrasive.

But the free movement through
elevated channels causes the scale to fold,
the council to abandon.

A Note on David Schubert

I'm feeling it now, sorrow
out of which to construct
some thing shining

         by a poet
whose quiet voice and sinewy
demeanor, the opposite
of sinewy minded

         are as comets
to a snowstorm, each has
its object neutralized
by its context so finding
out what that is

         is less important
than finding the next time
you can say it.

         Into the bargain
go fears and wishes like the
brains of a cow into a pot,
unremarkable and completely
convincing

　　　　　as when, in moments
of clarity dispensing its
sidewalks, I pull over
to the curb.

　　　　　The air is a compound
of air and peaches; air,
under and through the door,
dusting a row of pigeons.

THE YEAR OF THE OLIVE OIL

1989

SUNRISE WITH SEA MONSTER

Well, we either do it or we don't, as the pigeon said to the loaf of
    bread
doubling as the sky, that is, unaffectedly rocky and clay gray, the
    color of rocks
bordering but not reflecting oceans and in particular the one that
    finds its way here
every so often, though not right now; a function of light and
    surface qualities
such as polish, facet, regularity of design,
implied or announced mineral content, the ability to stand still in
    a storm,
and those qualities that enter surface and suffuse it, or melt
    suddenly
into the next-door apartment building, swept down into the back
    garden tow,
like transitions whether in writing or in music that aren't really
    transitional
so that cadence is a matter, ordinarily, of being stunned rather than
    construed,
but no diminishment, as in "fancy" and "open fifths" and
    "environmental sweepstakes"

LITTLE CAPE COD LANDSCAPE
for Darragh Park

The garbage is bagged, deposited in the dump, and several months later produces its interest, roses.

Late last night some people walking near the harbor were half-bagged and wanted to walk all the way out on the slippery jetty. Their roses were all talk, but they managed to accomplish their goal in spite of their questionable condition. Sleep roses, roses of the derailed train, rose roses and more roses.

THE YEAR OF THE OLIVE OIL
for Yuki Hartman

I sing the olive oil, I who lately sang
The clarinets in their sturdy packing case, the failure
Of the economy to be both seasonal and self-sufficient,
Packed off like cargo ships into the dim asperities of twilight.
Spread on Italian bread it became the summer sky—
And sometimes (brittle as failure) as musical as crystal.
One bottle contained all the arts. Another stimulated conversation
Which was itself the first pressing.
Darker pressings for the night
And each dawn had its geographical nuances, French and Spanish
Greek and Syrian, as on overcast days there were lumps
Of tough, overworked dough, gray and suffocating, with just a
     trace of gloss.
Then success was measured in thinness like an expensive watch;
Failures were as muddy as colors mixed by an infant.
Even virtual sewing machine oil, rancid with use, had a place
Beside winters when spears of sunlight, like armed tears,
Fenced in flame-blue iris and more ingenious pupil.
There were kingdoms advertising their future connections
(In crystal palaces with silver flags, cork-like minarets)
Fields of long, slender wheat coated with spring rain:
Sharing with the Jams the flow of shade
And with the Glues and Ointments a calculator-like display

Of the forces of temperature and pressure, as on August days in
   city office buildings.
One type was restricted to the human body, as its perfection and
   condiment.
Before this, there would have been no adhesive
For the world scrape, no solution (admittedly fugitive).
Music caught in the throat like peanut butter
And chords were torn apart, something like peaceful war-resisters
Until there was little sense of connection.
People read and wrote in fits, misunderstanding the true nature of
   the medium.
Then or soon after the intellect was felt to be
A part of life's suspension, and barbers never had to oil
Their scissors. If there was an occasional
Domestic squabble, it ran to gentle advice.
It is clear that vegetables, as in Andrew Marvell, were the chief
Image and model of human desire; and like water off a duck's back
—Pressed to golden brown, with pale gold juices intact and *no*
   fat—
Slid the momentary chagrins and anxieties, the bankruptcies
Spiritual and otherwise—otherwise irremediable; except for
Long slow decanting like passages of pure virgin time.
They had, as far as I can see, no word for friction.
It looked like a partial though real changeover to ball bearings
On the part of even the most adamant faculties of mind and body,
Writer's cement block and fractious self-interest group (the quiet
   ferment

72

Made clear by the necessity to be glass-clad, stoppered)
Enabling human achievement to flourish like a gold breeze,
Circular and reforming in the glow and liquid fragment.

THE POSTCARD ELEMENT IN WINTER

1

Supposing the wildlife became a person
who suddenly sprouted into an infinite number of ideas
each idea casting an ideal glow from canyon to canyon
like the most wandering star

whose atmosphere singes the very park
—as though the city existed to be barreled through
in spite of the windy quiet on its face
the factory snap, the raw potatoes and practicing the bassoon

2

~~Your recent letter is so stupid so utterly moronic its~~
~~a little difficult to believe it was~~
~~written by a human being let alone someone~~
~~who made it past the second grade you~~
~~miserable bastard do you eat~~
~~from a plate~~ thanks for your letter of January 5th
I enjoyed getting it

Prometheus at Fenway

Carl Yastrzemski, the Boston Red Sox outfielder/first baseman, and Prometheus, the carrier of fire and its related arts to humans, are tragic heroes in the Aristotelian sense of the term. Both are champions, both suffer reversals as a result of a mistake or character flaw inextricable from their greatness, and both are ultimately redeemed, though in different ways.

Prometheus the Titan, punished by Zeus for stealing fire from the Olympians and thereby saving humankind, suffers through many lifetimes chained to a rock in the unpleasant Caucasus. Each day a vulture or eagle gnaws at his liver, and each day the liver grows back. Rather than repent or try in any way to placate the god, Prometheus is defiant throughout, thereby adding greatly to his difficulties. Carl Yastrzemski, in the modern Caucasus of baseball, improves his strength at a gymnasium one winter and the next season leads the American League in batting average, home runs (tied) and runs batted in. The Red Sox, proverbially good "on paper" and wilting in the strong sun of September, are saved from their reputation and win the American League Pennant. At the height of his powers, trying to make the extraordinary usual, Yastrzemski begins to swing for the fences, sees his average, home runs and RBI's fall off dramatically, and the Red Sox go eight years minus a reminder of their flare of glory. His fans silently plead with him to meet the ball, but he continues to swing so hard he nearly falls down.

Prometheus literally (or semi-literally) and Yastrzemski figuratively are chained to their errors-cum-excellence: in Prometheus' case a strong sense of Self tinted by a rather stubborn self-righteousness (mitigated, it must be said, by the encouraging knowledge that he will live to see his tormentor's downfall); in Yastrzemski's case an unreliably expanded Self-image, possibly helped along by an inflated salary. This is before "free" agency. Prometheus eventually emerges free and victorious, a model, among early role-models, for humans. Yastrzemski returns to his real strengths: singles and doubles; skillful running, fielding and throwing, plus a flare for the extraordinary in all three; and a sense of his limits as player, person and hero, helping the Red Sox to their third pennant drive (stalled in the World Series) and ensuring himself via skill and "longevity" of a place in baseball's Hall of Fame in Cooperstown, N.Y.

"Carl" is a form of "Charles," which is a form of "chain." Both Southampton and the Caucasus are difficult to farm (though each produces its own memorials: time- and space-bound myth, potatoes, paintings, the rarer virtues of necessity). Yastrzemski left Notre Dame after his first year, finishing up later at Merrimack; Prometheus never went to college, but showed good insight especially concerning others, the courage of his convictions, and that pranks can be more important than they initially appear. Yastrzemski isn't a big man by sports standards; Prometheus gained and lost every day.

In point of fact, Fenway Park has been a *tragic floor* for better than fifty years, in spite of—and in part because of—those exceptional years 1967, 1975 and 1946, and the well known generosity of the late Irishman Tom Yawkey. The Green Monster is Boston's vulture, each day tearing out the hearts of its passionate fans many of whom live in and around New York and returning them dramatically the next. Batting third in their respective lineups, in the prime of their lives, neither Prometheus nor Yastrzemski can quite locate the "UP" elevator of Fortune. Yastrzemski strikes out by over-swinging; Prometheus can't even take a shower. Both were originally from the tip of Long Island but not Southampton proper. Both had a mission from the time the atmosphere was distinctly semi-pro. Both were booed. Yet each developed an exterior that was tough *and* appealing: a gritty appeal: resolution and independence and more than a hint of helpless pig-headedness, tempered by a complete absence of the usual self-interest (as evidenced, among other things, by Yastrzemski's relatively moderate superstar salary, Prometheus' almost callous disregard for his own welfare); or certainly no more than is usual, merging at all points with the larger concerns of the group in a rare display of *knowledge* and *power* so unaffectedly conjoined that Yeats who naturally comes to mind begins to embarrass with his "elevated horniness" and questions designed to take the reader's mind off the real issue ("loosening thighs").

Each expands in time or something like it: Yastrzemski merging with the single-minded, almost too brilliant, driven and childlike whipped brilliance of Ted Williams and on back to the folly of Babe Ruth; Prometheus undergoing metamorphosis after metamorphosis, expanding and contracting both (in the heroic mode of the Incredible Shrinking Man, whose resonance and overview are in inverse proportion to his gradual diminishment), beyond the incredible folly of his brother Epimetheus towards the undiminished atoms of Lucretius and Democritus, until it is obscure whether there is a universe apart from the chorus of scintillae that impinge on our competitive painterly consciousnesses guaranteeing our apparent freedoms, as against their dark green, almost black background and still darker energy source, running the turf of our years.

TINKER TO EVERS TO RANDOMNESS

Most of matter is space; and
the spatial is a kind of industrial
solvent always being offered at
a discount, like new shopping malls
      forever unfolding
      newer ones, which stretch
      not the ideal land- or air-rights
      but the modern account (like a series
      of transparent mailboxes each of
      which holds a future at
      least in potential); which is
      not to say that quartz-like
      there are no urban creatures to shine, or
that out of the blue the urban moonlight
fills the canyons as against the
sheer idea of technique, windblown
skidding like our wildest dreams.

A NOTE TO TONY TOWLE (AFTER WS)

One must have breakfasted often on automobile primer
not to sense an occasional darkening in the weather joining art
    and life;
and have read *Paradise Lost* aloud many times in a Yiddish accent

not to wake up and feel the morning air as a collaborator
thrown from some bluer and more intelligent planet
where life, despite the future's escalating ambitions, has ramified

in every direction except UP; and have been asleep a long time
in the air bonded to night not to feel the force of the present
shimmering in the downtown buildings, like European walled
    cities

whose walls have all but disappeared via benign invasion
and touristic drift, even the World Trade Center
for all the enigmas concerning *who* is trading *what* to *whom,*

and while deracination is fast qualifying as essence
rather than attribute, towards the brush with open sea.

APRIL

To normal seeing, a cloud that is also known,
as to the air branches are contrast as well as harmony.
Time is one answer, but space has a will of its own.

Thus when we say anything is *known*
we mean the air supporting it (sometimes violently,
to normal seeing the cloud that is also known)

is moved by what was formerly known
to disclose its presence, even indistinctly.
Time is one answer, space has a will of its own.

If it verges on the separation between known
and knower, the moving back and forth not exactly
spatial and even less in time (normal seeming plus known clamor)

then seeing takes place regardless of what is or isn't known—
seeing air like this, on the verge of entity
time being one answer, space having a will of its own.

Which will flowering as though on its own
(while the sun burns and powders over the burned-in city)
is normal seeing, a cloud that is also known
if time is one answer, if space has a will of its own.

A Note on Labor Day
For Paula

Sometimes I think I'm
close to discovering
why half my life has occurred
in a fog, which makes
the other half radiant
by comparison.
The wind,
September's ship,
blows some pigeons
out of a blue and white voiceless fog
off the cornice. Another
flock, atmospherically vague,
is flowing east: a rather pale gleam
with fragments of a greenish metal
embedded in it, among
them a starfish complete
with notes on its history.
Musical ones.
And I seem to be
lost again, if that doesn't
sound too dramatic,
and this time seems worse,
or around the slightly silvered bend

slightly blurred in late sun
that has some whirling filters over it
mostly for the jackets and the books.
The cars
stay close to the ground
to be near the trucks.
The busses and taxis move heaven
and earth to be near anyone.
And a green chair floats heavily
to earth smelling like burning leaves,
crushing some Americans
who were unwilling to work.
Armless, legless and backless
chairs—ah your back, that field.
If picture-taking
is discussed at all
and it isn't, the notes
go up in smoke—from
a wood fire, thick and concealing nothing.
The sky gets off its cot;
shoves some pamphlets into the giant blue hand
(the way Nixon pushed Ziegler)
holding the drink,
as mindless as mindless city planning.
A school of fish passes in the bright sunlight,
a bicycle is stolen and lofted
into the chilly air over Riverside Park,

sentenced to be held without trial
each afternoon succumbing
to the green of each evening
with no hope of putting it off.
Sirens whoop and swallow the earth.
Indigestible!
And flat!
To lie along its surface, walk
around as we all do
even the Flatiron Building—
in the middle of the general
unresolve that untangles
itself once a day to hang
just outside the windowsill,
somewhat humiliated,
like dusk, and caring
only in wildly scattered notes.
So a tugboat has plowed
up Broadway pulling half
the Battery behind it
and a moving van roars by, throwing
minor problems into far-flung relief
except for a barking dog which heaves
a luminous sigh...too explosive
still, for the pigeons,
but thick enough
to cover the peeling paint

and traffic passing, passing
under cover of dusk
which was the underpainting of its wish.
The pen being an extension
of the arm, coffee rushes
into it, saved from dislocation
by some purple flames at the top: accompanied
by a kind of fugue starting
in the sewers—alligator youth band
plus a few bright rats to fill
out the strings, ah music—
as a testimonial
mostly confused
to Brahms sentinel and chief persuader
(vice-president Jean Siméon Chardin,
secretary Andrea Palladio) as that
snowy city piles on others and
the process rapidly reverses, like
the Falls at St. John's,
which are to this bright late day as blue
to peaked snow. Of the twelve
ways to success, one
is not taking the window
off its sash and throwing
it down onto the street, where
it crashes like a tennis racket
onto the head of an Australian

who took a wrong turn.
Like an awkward, but
awkwardly staying dream;
that the dream is always in
Spanish, always held over,
throwing the air across the way
into mental confusion like a surprise
quiz, on the entire planet
of reference, with terracing
on all sides to provide a quick aisle,
visually, to accidents,
bank robberies, lovers' quarrels (stabbing
at the corner leaving about
fifty yards of blood)
and holiday quiet, withdrawn
and hardly able to speak
though not from not wanting to,
the way the roof separates
exaggeratedly revealing the moon,
with yellow hair, worn
close and tied at the
back into a kind of ponytail,
with a tortoise-shell barrette, to
make you easier to find.
And a subway stumbles
clatteringly on into the night
carrying the hopes and fears of absolutely no one.

Instead, a suspended life burying
its head in the paper, or paper bag,
together with a cockroach
the size of a small dog, who
comes forward occasionally
to sample the cooking and the clothes
or carves a road on someone's
stranded wakefulness, to confuse matters
further. Now the coffee is gone,
like the pigeons, back
into the cannon until
some backfire or genuine shooting
sends them crashing off
the roof in an avalanche of
domestic tranquillity scattered
to the four winds—
with lips that part sometimes
to stagger the imagination, like
Aphrodite's breasts. Ships,
brilliant apartment buildings facing west
all the purposes and prospects
none of which are mine, how can
I be so frantic as I sometimes
seem, or do I want to be
thought so, and by whom.
And by whom not, talking
not to talk, to distract

the orders who have our mouths and lingual structure
—or yours, you critical schmuck.
Trees wave on the roof
across the street
which has the forsythia for two weeks
every year, which I always want you
to paint, which is past,
or almost, as light sweeps it
diagonally across the frontier
between reality and metaphysics, with some
early fall smells for a walking stick.
Metaphysics takes
strong exception—fortunately
it speaks only German, and stutters.
If someone is hammering
below, smoothing out our street,
no one is fixing coffee in
a room gradually filling with paintings,
each transforming the room into
an awareness of its lack,
or mine, leaving music
as the prime consolation for the inability
to leave the body, except insofar
as music throws off her clothes
to reveal her secret self:
the absence of a secret.
Such a metallic light on that roof—like

braces on a rabbit.
People crawl to work,
crawl to lunch, crawl to coffee break,
crawl to the subway, and the bin
and home, its obscured
vision lately like a meadow
overwhelmed by goldenrod, among the more
disturbing and radiant overtones, and a
newspaper weighted with cement
cracks against the garage door
and stars are catapulted across
the lawn to catch on the telephone wires: banded
with lindens in a reverse twist
as if the air were
a part of the earth, and waking
required only a slight elevation.
Every twenty minutes.
Which means getting up
from the couch (spinning)
and seeing the sky radically changed
from its previous appearance
—like a gull that dropped
through the 7 stages of life
in a single afternoon—
as a giant clam pushed slowly
over Riverside Park, in mild hopes
of dinner under the stars,

its muscles gradually faltering
though not without a certain
pleasure in being eaten by
discriminating people who chose
this time and place to appear in.
Or not to disappear from.
The ocean is mainly a difference
in scale—sun streaking
boards in preference to sky
whose spangling is threatening to take
over the earth—allowing for
vacation time, thunderheads,
insect bites, the pull of
work and the rest. Sleep
douses it like so much dust to be swept.
Meanwhile the building, shaded
lighter towards the top,
has been picked up and deposited
in another warp, suffering
mainly from reference shock,
with only the books and
records intact, as predicted
by several of them.
The light changes state.
Changes again.
The animals have done
only half the work which has

to be completed by nightfall
and the teams are warming up.
A weasel (?) just emerged from the clubhouse
carrying a woman. Critics chase both away.
Traveling at the speed of light
to be elsewhere, in the dream
which is the subject of Spanish poetry
or the *which*, which seems French . . .
your hair lagging behind your cheek
the pupil is flushed and held
accountable for the darker haze
of its surroundings, which is night
taking my breath away.

LOOKING AT THE BRIGHTER NIGHT

You get to feel the limits of framing, not unlike
Charles the Bad (d. 1387) who having been sewn into
a sheet soaked with brandy by doctors who thought
alcohol a panacea, and who then held up a lit candle . . .
the idea being that form proclaims
the *formless*, regardless of night and its celebrated reductions
linking all things to their proper names,
Bar des Bouquinistes et Filles aux Cheveux de Lin,
Cheap Passage to Natchez, Harborside Cock
and Pullet (England); O city tromboned beyond its poles

For a Cowper Paperweight

Not that his writing isn't moving when
it doesn't seem it should be,
owing in part, at least, to the cloud of difficulty
surrounding his difficult life,
the pleasure of the low key
and mastery of cadence—but that it is
difficult to say why some of it
should be as good as it is, the life
of the writing apart from the life.
The quiet assertions made,
assertion becomes an extended lyric
which, foregoing rapture (as it foregoes
rhapsody) presents feeling in such
a way that it ascends human heights,
both detailing and depending on
the level motion of the feeling tone,
like a long headline broken up into
individual letters and presented
at random, one letter at a time
throughout long and occasionally tedious
narrative and description, the promise of sunshine
throughout a long brightly overcast afternoon.
(As though—almost—one had to compete
with the weather and lose in order

to feel anything, or as though mere utterance
blended one with what was being uttered,
in this case ground and sky, the nature
and numerous pleasures of being between.)
Nor do the exceptions in what prevails,
"I was a stricken deer, that left the herd
Long since; with many an arrow deep infixt
My panting side was charg'd," alter
the weather of the context, while lending a sense
of extra, unrepressed life to the whole;
to a whole consisting of dullness
as well as all the other neighboring kingdoms.
A sense that pleasure is often
pleasure of recognition which doesn't depend
on prior experience—though one has had that too.
"Oh Winter, ruler of th'inverted year,
Thy scatter'd hair with sleet like ashes fill'd,
Thy breath congeal'd upon thy lips, thy cheeks
Fring'd with a beard made white with other snows
Than those of age, thy forehead wrapt in clouds,
A leafless branch thy sceptre, and thy throne
A sliding car, indebted to no wheels,
But urg'd by storms along its slipp'ry way,
I love thee, all unlovely as thou seem'st,
And dreaded as thou art!"

Poem For Trevor Winkfield

Two mops are cavorting in the next world.
"What do you do?"
"Nothing! I don't do anything!"
Orange light, then darkness. Then orange light.

SONNET

The dream: to have
more time.
And suppose you could have all the time?
Someone walks up and deposits
in your outstretched hand,
not time exactly; but
of all that is circumambient,
all that pure aura, the infinite possibility
that although no one thing is lost
nothing is exceptional.
Leaves pry out the distance
between new construction and the old
bright lights, massed for waterfront
and mixed use alike. The painter
pulls back, shades his eyes.

FROM NOCTURNES

1

Suppose the impossible: that the *peeing* were the romantic part, and the *screwing* made everybody leave the room. Except you of course, and the night and its meteoric music. Persons skate by like undelivered (and undeliverable) groceries, freaked by discourse, as if that were a function of the charge: to board up windows in a skyscraper and have someone or some thing break through periodically. But the gods are drunk; and the large suitcases lining up until some threaten to be architecture, or at worst architectural sculpture, are inclining towards New Jersey; some semi-glittering en route.

2

As the Romantic contribution—that one sees oneself by perceiving landscape, since projection is the yew tree of life—thins out into the wash of latter-day psychoanalysis, so ornament during the time the light actively settles means what it says it means. The half-buildings in the narrow world have fallen asleep. A yellow light is emanating from the brain over the Hudson River. If you took up the visible threads and glued them, so they formed one dark gray thread with highlights that implied and also severed all connections, then the present roof together with its one-time cornice would enact the precise texture it needs from the virtual—it looks like a horizon—fragment above, outlasting along a different perspective line as the narrow world outlasts its own formations, the state of grace being fed by nothing so much as sheer presence.

3

The gods are fighting to stay awake. Just now one hurled something over the drawn-in end of the river below. Everything is subsumed, the sleep of landscape, the flowers in the window box existing when no one is looking, the street with its bone china and animadversions towards roots of daylight. Time stops gamely. A large bloodshot eye encircled by small gray cumulus clouds behind a white shade, a smudge near Mercury, twin towers at the far end of the spectrum, an inverted pyramid of cheese, tomatoes, and extra cheese. Moments hurtle through over and below open and closed windows scattering crystals, roars of houseplants. The far piling marbled with green and white light, transfixing the Northeast, is Discord.

CLARINET
>(after André Chénier)

Less than a recurrent dream, but more haunting.
The clarinet is poised and I begin playing,
conscious of occupying some exact center
where I am both rival and conqueror.
My usually awkward embouchure
produces tones which are inspired and pure.
Its fingers latch on to mine and hold on tight,
lifting and dropping them until *I* get it right,
over and over. As though beauty entered will,
brightening and darkening the resonant bell.

ON THE ROAD
(after Colin Muset)

And when I see winter coming on
I feel like staying put.
If I could find the right host
who had more than enough and didn't care,
books, records, a comfortable house in the country,
a lot of bread, a lot of cheese, and a lot of beer,
the kids happy, baseball just in case
and you beside me in the wilderness . . .
and if his wife is as generous as he is
and always thinks of my pleasure first,
days and nights for as long as I've been here
(with no hint of jealousy on his part,
no choosing not to leave us entirely alone)
then I would forget all about this writing business,
all the bad stretches and muddy turnings-off,
plus a lot of general unpleasantness besides.

People and Buildings

The answer is to be one with daylight,
which doesn't support the question. The light bends,
people and buildings are swept into the night

like shaved notions of ideas, bright
knowledgeable and containing countless addenda.
The answer is to be one with daylight.

Not that painting scalds everything to a white
brilliance in which to see means as true ends—
people and buildings are swept into the night

along with other versions of their tightly
organized consciousnesses, nerve ends.
The answer is to be one with daylight

which approaches along a slate of brightening
occurrence in which means and would-be ends
like people and buildings are swept into the night

to recur with meaning and occasional delight
of a piece with dawn and its staggered ends.
The answer is to be one with daylight
but people and buildings are swept into the night.

102

Fourteen Poems

Similarly; whereby the current polarization
Holds out little hope for lasting revision

★

Meanwhile tragedy outgrows its religious
Origins in an effort to encompass

★

A dip in air pressure, the sense that daylight
Has slipped from its porch onto the grassy night

★

Need, ambition, unrest, and one-dimensional
Thinking latticed on a horizon of metaphysical

★

Rather than its extension by mutual process
Into means, and thence the directory of endless

★

103

Aquamaniles used to come in colorful guises
People and monsters joined in practical devices

★

Is circuitous like memory in a snake.
You follow the coastline for several miles, then forsake

★

A large patch of dandelions, the sense that light
Has curled back into the eye—a *figment* of sight

★

A theory may be true and also a puzzle
As good weather includes an occasional light drizzle

★

Cartwheeled bolted to the explosion that worked
By individual decoy which for once unfrocked

★

The way "blue sky" is an appropriate term
Emitting a clear redundancy, like a germ

★

As beautiful as a jar that holds the Beautiful
For centuries—or until the *idea* is full

★

All landscape and consequently all distance
Are wings, to which the essential substance

★

Raspberries being the perverse lachrymae
Confusing time and space. As for civic decay

Baseball as a Fact of Life

A simulated pie crust of poured concrete, with pitchfork marks slicing through every so often to let sun and people in and out. Strips and bellies, pets and projects, peanut shells, vocalise—no! At the far end someone crouched, apparently examining something. As I watch he raises a hand to his cheek, rakes downward in a distinctly *unheimlich* maneuver; appears to unroll a strip of Scotch tape from under the rim of his fedora—in fact he's dressed rather nattily, somewhat in the manner of a 30s saxophone player—first around his hairline, then down around one side of his forehead, along the cheekbone and underneath his nose, which he scrunches down, while curling his upper lip up to hold the tape in place (giving that portion between upper lip and nostrils the air of a mostly transparent moustache which the wearer would, when all was said and done, be just as happy to have off; also an odd expression, something like that of a professional balloon blower), next feeding it into his mouth where he does something obscure with his tongue, out the other side and around his chin

all the while continuing his *lecture*—for that is what I am now aware his posture has signified from the start—on the faults, numbering in the legions, of my baseball lineups. I realize that what I have been taking all the while as concentration has been his utter and consummate displeasure at the quality, organization,

106

publication, copyrighting, and sheer space-displacement of a series of list poems I wrote some twelve years earlier, inspired (I hoped) by the nonpareil French poet Arthur Rimbaud. In an instant it is as though there is no "as though" about it: my entire life has been occupied by this dark room, I have no idea whether night follows day, whether the sun has ever in fact shone on the earth, or whether I have returned from my monthly trip to Lyons or am just starting out as tour guide on a new one.

★ ★ ★

This critic for *Cahiers du Cinéma*, whom I will call Arthur, is wonderful at devastating my movie lineup. For some odd reason *The Baker's Wife* by Marcel Pagnol is the most heinous inclusion, and among the capital sins of omission Italian movies of the 60s, the very thought of them, sends him into paroxysms of rage. I try—*not* to defend my selections, which to me was never the point, those being as often as not the given, the world among other versions of it, so that arranging them in baseball terms deranges the same world; while rearranging it, I dared to hope, in an outrageous but valid way, valid (if at all) the way the teenage years are valid: *cleat-like*: both, as F.T. Prince might say, leave a skid mark.

"You don't know anything *about* American baseball!" I shout. "You don't even know how to pronounce the word!"

But by this point he no longer seems to notice my presence, much less take in my protestations in his fourth or fifth language, EFL, and the theater has begun to whir and sputter, the prelude to an explosion. I am about to shout something further about his *world-wide* ignorance of both baseball and movies

—I am, for example, the only one in the universe who knows he originally forged his press card, and that although born in France in some obscure *département* known only for its boots and fragrant nights, he speaks only phonetic French, lip-synching, when he can manage that, to a cassette player he wears underneath the back of his shirt collar like the Marx Brothers with their Maurice Chevalier imitations in *Monkey Business*, the collaborator on permanent skids—barely enough, in fact, to make it past the ushers in the moonlight cinémathèque in whatever town he happens to be conceptualizing in, and often finding his seat by the purest of pure chance—

when he turns and from evident light years away fixes me with the most penetrating and blinding stare I have ever encountered.

★ ★ ★

The street outside is quiet now save for an occasional cough, a tardy dog wandering among loose scraps and peels of conversation. I am holding my breath, in both hands, locked somehow in the swollen moment which is time illuminated, when his cheek

goes pink
then scarlet
while unearthly sounds stir
from some impenetrable
coign in his being
as though the blood
circulating through his major organs
has turned to uncut rubies

"I'll—!"

I am about to say, to my later and infinite humiliation, that I am
willing to *edit*, at least the movie lineup, when I am stopped in
my mental tracks. He is now in profile, hunched over as I first
witnessed him, his entire being involved in whatever has produced
his current mental and physical state, which has begun to produce
in me a tinge of sympathy along with the antipathy one naturally
feels towards sheer evil or self-promotion ("Good news! I've just
come out with the definitive book in your field!"), with the same
thin strip of curling tape proceeding mysteriously from his hat,
underneath his nose, and towards the bottom of his facial structure.

An international movie, with titles and credits from five or six
nations, fans out from his one blinding eye I can see, framed
by his head now dark gray and metallic, to the wall opposite,
through a small window, and out into the night across a pitch-
black street to another wall belonging to an unprepossessing

building standing among others of mixed use. Within the triangle thus formed by eye and radiating light, all dust and glow, a great many people are standing in line before a doorway, among them Michelangelo Antonioni, Federico Fellini, Ingmar Bergman, Alfred Hitchcock, Marcel Carné, Jean Renoir, Alain Tanner, Akira Kurosawa, and Jerry Lewis, together with the two typical Englishmen from *The Lady Vanishes*, Ray Bolger in his farmer's overalls, Jean Simmons wet from the Glory version of *Blue Lagoon*, Randolph and Lizabeth Scott, Eddie Constantine— and the line is moving forward slowly and evenly without diminishing into the low, light gray building. The sun comes out bright and warm overhead.

Pan bagna vendors stroll this way and that on the paved walk lining the beach. Across the boulevard a small dinner party is being given for the *monstres* of modern cinema. The air is a sea of garlic, soupe au pistou, bouillabaisse. Seagulls and car horns. Many of the greatest figures of the auteur era, the pre-auteur era, and post-auteur California ("There's much too much snew in the second reel." "What's *snew*?" "Nothing much. What's new with you?") and, strangest to say, someone who looks exactly like Allen Funt wearing full catcher's gear—although, to be perfectly candid, Allen Funt looked a good deal like my father at a particular time in the mid-life of both, a period spanning as much as fifteen years; until both men inextricably involved with their cameras and their spools begin to merge not so much with each other as with the silent rapid free-float of non-poetic

110

images from brightness to the mobile dark, with the additional help of an appreciative audience weaned on *8½* and the cast of the original *M★A★S★H*, infinitely and uncritically dark and still—or if in motion obscurely so while the lights continue to flicker, bright and dark as day.

NEW AND SELECTED POEMS

1999

What Is Said to the Poet

concerning the impieties of obscurity
and the dark flurry
to the left of the water tower
providing the state with a pre-emptive sea
      cantilevered over what you
      can see. I would like to be
      the grain elevator of all I see
      but the last slice of sea
      outlining the observatory
      has cleared up the cooperative
      conversion process, windows
      fighting a rear-guard
action to sort out clarity
from its numerous self-styled conservators.
And architects hoist space underneath
timber roofs, producing the clerestory.

French Notebook Threatened By Writing

1. The day is broader than the night though more foreshortened.

2. The moon sleeps in its fully realized breadbasket.

3. For they exit via a kind of enchanted lobby pulling down
   housing starts—still housing starts have made something
   of a recovery if not nearly enough.

4. Even now your breath is volcanic to this music it sounds like
   Mozart—or very early Beethoven.

5. Fields with a thin winter glaze on them above and beyond.

6. The day is broader than the night.

7. The moon sleeps in its fully realized breadbasket.

THE DAWN

The dawn was contagious, spreading
rapidly about the heavens. —Flann O'Brien

TO BE

Immortal.

ONLY

A pencil line of sunlight is climbing
Straight up the chimney, stopping about two inches
From the top

IMPINGING

On a template of powder blue without end

IT FOLLOWS THAT

Compressed, highlighted and seductively polished
Within a naturally limited theater of operations
Snow or sleet, the occasional burst rising to produce
A new century

SPACE IS FURIOUS

Still beneath the roof of your hair
The dials keynote our penchant for constructing
Problems that test the ground underneath, reflecting wintergreen
All the way up to buildings including several different varieties

THE WAY IT PRODDED

All nabis and all
Oily charm, conveniently summarized
Which is not to say without vague hopes of escape into the
    evening sky

PARTICULARLY THE DAWN

Approximately fifteen feet back from where
The houses, secure at least temporarily from flattening,
Peered out over what had been left of the horizon—that is,
What hadn't been previously usurped
By the "developers"

WHEN LAST WE

Met.

EVEN NOW

Your arms are the unencumbered coastline

LIKE AN ALTO SAXOPHONE

With cherries in the bell. It isn't
Selected cities

LIMNING

And individuating green light; as though some passing cloud

SOFTER THAN LASERS TO STYROFOAM

Not exactly carried aloft like the anthem of autumn
But a rubric of sopping wet air that
Has aimed its complement in a forthcoming way

A SWEET SMELL

Like the armpit
Of an angel

OR PERFECTION OF THE LIFE

The earth is

Pulled up to the surface, or
The surface is pulled down till it hits; either way
The blue is spooned over lush

WHY I AM NOT A GERMAN ROMANTIC

THE PLACE OF RUNNING BOARDS

If, and it's a big one,
This clumsy desire to be confined to you and you only
Means hammering out the decision
Where all is difficult to see

AS THOUGH EACH FRAGRANT CAUSEWAY

Doubled the space between monsters—I mean trampling
The news from the perspective of summer
Until the only boarder of note sheds quality
In the form of clothespins pushed up towards the thinnest leaf

NOT BEING OR BEING NOT BEING

The primroses

OF MY DISCONTENT

Not the shoal

Where we argue the limitless side, but somehow
Swarming down the coal chute to be played
According to those golden notions of equal
And opposite reaction, swallowed up by, at least
In part, the same religious architecture
That works on the mind like feelers, extending even into the
    current

LIKE CARROTS TO HILLS

The gray carrots, and the almost
Maple rolling hills

SHOOTING FOR LINE

for Bob Hershon

To break the silence or your newly acquired Ming vase,
or raise my expectations and the flag over the Brooklyn Navy Yard.
To employ a veritable army of secretaries, or your for once awake
    faculties
in coming to grips with the enemy, the notion that nothing out-
    lasts our fleeting perception of it
in addition to reflecting on the newly painted wall and what just
    transpired,
slurred speech and the passage from the Schumann
permitting some liberties, the picnic to go on as originally
    scheduled.

If you paint the garage door green, yourself into a corner
(to stagger home at midnight, the times people come and go from
    work)
it may be to place objects in the memory, the lips on the hard
    rubber mouthpiece
before turning the room upside down, a deep scarlet.
Meanwhile changing to life-support or funky black-tie
is a far cry from poisoning the drinks or good names
of those who fly Cessnas or the banners of dubious political loyalty
in the name of something higher or Benedict Arnold,
or cutting to the chase, an armful of her favorite wildflowers.

And yet the fall is precipitous, warmer than in any of the six
    preceding years.

To rewrite the book on how to be obnoxious in public and
    Stéphane Mallarmé.
Once you are involved in the institutional end of the arts and her
    lustrous hair,
it isn't to pinpoint excess, the exact spot where the light appears to
    transcend itself.
It is possible to run in circles or a decent-sized refrigerator business
without diffusing all of your energies, a greenish blue ink through
    ordinary tap water,
or paying out bonuses every Christmastime, the fishing line over
    the rippling pond . . .
I mean, to count your real blessings, how many stars make up
    the Little Dipper;
open the door to the shed or an account at the local bank
so that attention can be paid, the overdue electric bill.

Whoso list to hunt and the names in the beat-up address book
I know better, contract law in the state of Idaho.
To respond to the veiled plea or unusual stimuli
carries with it an obligation to be human, a satchel containing
    the proceeds for that week
serving a dual purpose and all who may have been kept waiting
as a result of the air traffic controllers strike, a hopefully
temporary abandonment of the notion of quality.

To lap the ailing runner or the dish of milk,
bask in Florida sun and her praise,
coming to New Jersey on Jan. 16, innumerable times like a hot
  pan of popcorn.

Still to consider changing jobs or popular fiction in light of the
  new and highly suggestive deconstructive techniques.
Who doesn't seek to improve basic reading skills or the land,
write off a fair-weather friend or a sequel to *War And Peace*?
It isn't rehashing the past, yesterday's shepherd's pie,
to blow the whistle on the funeral industry, the wet shutters
  seemingly all night long—
to endow her with more than the eye can see, a small liberal
  arts college
to the tune of $300 million and "Hail to the Chief"
touching most major side issues and the place where scar tissue
  had substantially healed,
or ruling the letterhead paper and what is in reality an
  extremely small fiefdom
to hit the nail on the head, a "frozen rope."
To divide your love equally or anything but a prime number,
lose your balance or your index cards;
or single you out from all others, through the drawn-in infield

while moving heaven and earth, the carefully crated stemware.
It opens new doors, the season of mists
and mellow fruitfulness. Pen the hogs; your last will and testament

relating to the issue under advisement, your mother's side:
to catch the meaning and/or Walter Johnson
colored by unconscious associations and the barely discernible
    tints of February's
trial balloon by long forgotten ordeal.

In short, we hold certain truths to be self-evident but the
    answers in code in the glove compartment,
and they eat up the presumed distance and the leftovers
like an unenacted crime bill or Sophocles' *Oedipus at Colonus*.
It seems likely that no one leaves *all* hope behind, a calling card
    fringed in tears and a raised border
but the wounds are bathed in salt, also the cocker spaniel.
It is taking not prisoners but a glass of red wine,
prendre un verre mais aucun prisonniers
bei mir bist du schön but you also block out the reading light
in which an axc is being sharpened, my appetite for new
    experience

making up for lost time and ghost stories to tell to the kids on
    Halloween.
The truck rolled up the kilometers, down the steep incline.
Sometimes taming a wild horse or an uncontrollable urge
can lead to unlooked for results, a battalion into a no-win
    situation
proving the guilt of those accused, particularly flimsy.
Wake up the sleeping giant, those planning to leave bright and

early before breakfast,
or fly in the face of conventional wisdom 500 miles north to
    Saskatchewan
for the solution to appear, sun through dense fog
dispersing warmth and shadows of telephone poles
as habits die hard, hornets sprayed with Raid.
It used to be filling an Angora sweater and a rackety DeSoto
to shadow your memories and the branch-haunted garage
    door,
what used to be called hope, or Brenda,
leaving aside questions of good taste and muddy shoes
to make for the hideout concealed behind dense shrubbery, a
    potentially dangerous enemy.
So it meant pulling the plug on candor and the black-and-
    white TV set.
I'm warming up to you, the macaroni and cheese in the toaster
    oven.
All in all, I find myself elbowing the impatient tourist and
    incipient greed
out of the way, Bed o' Roses by Man o' War,
while they skate mostly on thin ice, the plans and those with
    rented blades,
time borrowed and old Benny Goodman records,
rounding things off to the nearest 100 and the corner on two
    wheels

126

to snap up the latest hit, you out of your pool of lethargy.
Meanwhile to compete with your cheekbones and a phantom
the sun burns fair skin and sometimes bridges,
let me not sing doo-wop or the raptures of never knowing
      enough about you;
or if new opportunities spring up and occasionally wild dogs
it pays to look managerial, the runner back to first base.
In light of winter and your extreme position
it seems best to avoid rhyme, entanglements of all kinds.
How many gloomy outlooks or peeling sills are painted
to reveal the inevitable, a view of barges in the Hudson
without assigning all of Hart Crane and their real property
and thus realigning priorities and tires grown threadbare
like the solution to a nonexistent puzzle, sodium chloride in a
      liter of Scotch,
so that the temptation to take a drink, provide a quick fix,
takes a back seat to language, the mature driver?

Gather up ye goatherd gods and your wits
which have fallen on the gym floor, our distinctly hard times.
When the sun sinks its nail into the boards of earth

the approach is cloudy, by way of the town dump.
Put out the cat, and then put out the cat.
Then it fell out, hair and what was portended,
that some trusted to luck, the self-styled family advisor

bestowing largesse of a kind and the kids on the grandparents
for the entire weekend.
How to play the Barber piano sonata or the tricky futures
market
without driving yourself crazy, 12 hours without stopping,
speaking volumes and the "degree" speech from *Troilus And
Cressida?*
For you can break the bank or its dark green shaded windows,
attack inefficiency or an undefended knight
while spending more than you earn in a year, your semen like
Don Juan.
This is keeping the tempo honest, an herb garden out of the
shadow of the air conditioner,
farming rocky soil and half the copy-editing
to avoid stress-related illness of all kinds or an onrushing
locomotive;
or take Ibuprofen tablets every 4 hours plus the not so subtle hint
to correct the condition as well as each major sentence error
to move the greatest number of readers, the computer table
over near the window
shaded by a thin curtain and the deepening afternoon.
If the answer falls on deaf ears or short of satisfying,
it only serves the lowest common denominator, a tennis ball
right over the wire fence,
dying on the vine, or in your arms
as Keats proposed to do and Fanny Brawne,
remembering the Alamo and the toothpaste.

To conclude: rooted in good loamy soil and the Lockean
    doctrine of individual rights,
firing the old flintlock and the watchman,
shooting for line or at the absolute outside the middle of next
    March.
If you push your luck or the dangerous passed pawn all the
    way to the eighth rank
it may help to collect items from the suggestion box, your wits
    where they still lie,
effectively closing the book and the prolonged meeting.
It amounts to the same: larding lectures with factitiously
    appealing anecdotal material
or the beef with fat despite consequences to the arteries.
Or you can put your stamp on the postcard or postmodern
    American poetry
or motion to the auctioneer for an adjournment
to lend an air of April and your very best blue suit:
sweep the minefield clear and all the accumulated dust into the
    corner.

DETAIL

Actually the idea of representing
putting one foot where the other
can't possibly go has always
seemed fragile at best
       and as for *this*
       standing in for always,
       the rowboat funding serpentine
       darknesses, even what won't
       change can't be said to be
       other than it looks like
       to us as we account for it,
       leaving the position of auditor
not to say guarantor up for grabs like
stars on a windy night, and any and all
vestiges of allegiance in tracks made
by snowshoes, of by and for the moment's loss

SONG

I am pressed up against you
Like air pressed up against the sky
The carpenter ants are at work on the bearing beams
O bearing beams

Like air pressed up against the sky
So will the hills attain
O bearing beams
Disguised as cows touched here and there with stray sunlight

So will the hills attain
Their dole of cloud-famished city
Disguised as cows touched here and there with stray sunlight
In short we frequently get tangled

Their dole of cloud-famished city
Each bordering river inflects with something of its own
In short we frequently get tangled
Which has nothing on confusion itself

Each bordering river inflects with something of its own
Sticking piecemeal above the regret
Which has nothing on confusion itself
Save that it lowers the boom on customary behavior

Sticking piecemeal above the regret
The word I have for you flowers in several places
Save that it lowers the boom on customary behavior
Like October's fiery rip

Aug.–Dec. for Jimmy Schuyler

8/3

Dense fog during the night and early morning. Late yesterday you could see it begin to flow and flatten back against the cliff of the Berkshires, very white and dreamlike. Most of today wet but bright—then at about 4:30 PM everything went suddenly black with violent rain for about 10 minutes. Virtually no cars on the big roads. Now, approaching dinner, it's unearthly, silent, bare, ships, towers, domes open unto late sun making it through a low ceiling like a tablecloth with stains and cigarette burns. Long cedar shadows look like they were just painted: a trio of robins advancing a few pecks at a time getting their feet wet.

8/5

Cold colors do not make you a cold person. Winter employs cold colors. Therefore winter is not a cold person.

8/7

For some reason the great drought isn't much in evidence, if you trust what comes in via the senses. Some brown patches here and there with currents of green flowing calmly through them; but almost all the trees look healthy, respiration normal, rate of circulation normal, no visible cysts or lesions.—Perhaps this is a *symbolic* drought? The butter-and-eggs were flown in direct from Normandy, the breeze is blowing, though what grass there is lies perfectly still beneath the stirred petals.

8/13

The apple trees—this is mid-*August*—are quietly, awkwardly spectacular: graduated in abutting fields from the fully human and operational to fledglings of 3 or 4 different sizes.

Late afternoon landscape with grassy dome, farm pond (with 2 large outcroppings near the center), cylindrical bales of hay, oaks and willows, maples, Constable shagginess and highlightings, and the dead en route: deer, raccoons, chipmunks, skunks, a venturesome chicken, an occasional bird—like the one that hit the windshield and popped up and back onto the road only without a pop. For a second it seemed as though nothing had happened and the bird was simply flying off in another direction, as surreal, or unreal, as the local speed limits.

—A Constable, with a Hopper parked in the middle of it.

8/14

Dawn, or a monarch butterfly. Cow mooing its tail off, followed by a rooster and various birds, all in D major. Artificially cool, the sky draped rather loosely but pinned down wherever the potential for disturbance exists (prickly ridge, electric wires, a 150-year-old giant oak gnarled and distorted, etc.). Buzzing and rattling, not yet burning.

The new lilac has an aura already, despite or possibly because of its being dwarfed by so much cedar in front behind in back

134

above below [desire mine]. The cedars, to give them their due, are perfectible: the problem is that the air is already perfect and taking up almost all the space.

It's interesting how every hum could be a plane, an approaching storm, a truck, a hornet, a sign of roadwork, but not the sea. The seas have dried up and embed splinters that were once demisemiquavers.

8/17
Coral is far more pinkish violet than the sky's undercoating, yet you exceed the shadows on the railing caused by intermittent breeze through the chewed up—thanks to the deer—juniper. The red has vanished close to the top and your scattering through the changeable filaments amounts to an infusion which, if its episodes were piled, would reach all the way to the telephone wires, fleeting and on record for its fleetingness.

8/18
Shadows being a literal commentary on things—

8/19
Underneath the sky is a single snow-dark cloud with no visible
     means of support
fortunately it doesn't have to hold anything up self o self
unfortunately the deer left in a rush taking Scotch bottles of Queen
     Anne's Lace with them

fortunately without unduly influencing the wet grass
at present an idea in the mind of the sky minus a controlling self
but nonetheless responsible for its actions among them an attentive
   disrespect

8/25

The hornet: now you see it now it sees you.

Apropos of which, every once in a while a pair of them scramble and slide noisily down a steeply pitched fiberglass roof. Are they fighting? copulating? From underneath, it's like watching a black & white cowboy movie on an old TV set, where the fight starts before the bad guy is unhorsed. And besides the "snow," the forms are uncanny. And *noisy*.

9/2 (NYC)

The second of two brilliantly conceived if overpoweringly humid days. Still light at 8:00 PM, west windows brighter than the sky whose uneasy deep blue-gray might have signaled a thunderstorm, were it not already evening and miles away from trunks bending and seeming to crack in the wind.

After Fairfield Porter (& for Rackstraw Downes): If you're a lousy poet you'll be a lousy poet if you write in forms and a lousy poet if you write without forms. If you're an interesting poet you'll be an interesting poet whether you use forms or don't use them!

9/3

One of those days edging so far over into undifferentiation that *Fate* appears to be entering on all sides.

On all fours.

9/4

The Mistress of the Cloudy Bright.

Describe an object so that its dullness is its virtue. If you have time, describe the same object so that it is at one remove, the dullness leaking out like helium from the best kept balloon. Be sure to leave time before during and after you write. The sky has so much gray woven into it that blue seems a thing of the past—beyond the striking and ultimately insupportable notion that all is in the past, courtesy of our perceptual workings and all they would embrace.

9/5

Like the Charm to the migraine, which has absolutely no use for it.

9/22

I finally have it. The *raccoons* are the intellectuals. The ducks, pigeons, frogs, mosquitoes, etc., get along on contrivance. Now I am going to commence reading as a duck, noting shore points, wind points, half-gainers into brackish pond water—till precipitation part me from my feathers.

The big trees bypass dusk on the way to the county seat. Smells and sounds of burning. And Natural Reticence enters, her hair aglow with chrysanthemums.

9/30

A clear cool day with no wind to speak of. The important buildings elevated just enough for light to pass underneath forming a human chain, air to people to air.

10/1

Withering, humidity, some Cubism (following a spectacular fall day blowing all over the place).

I get a kick out of the critical shibboleth of "poetic development." As though by assuming there is "mature" work you can then point backwards to what is assumed to have set the stage for it, demonstrating the assumed qualities the latter is assumed to lack.—Or perhaps kick isn't precisely the word.

I would like to say something to the clouds that simply hang there without an outline to their name. Snowy, caught on projections, pushing hard against substance. No underside darkening. Appearing to shimmer. Clustered around a Nouvelle Usine apartment house stuck up on the Palisades with a cloudy glue. Like a turkey with a secret glowing inside it.

Goldberg Variations. Gulled Birk, Cold Burg, Guild Bug, Galled Bike, Gllld_____Bhrrkgkcccgg.

10/2

It's not the leaves per se, and not lines, but rather *handfuls* and *carloads*.—Also mounds, lozenges, partial sphcres, snifters, wedges, ziggurats, domes, secants, bales, mortal arches.

10/14

Columbus Day. The vexed person and not the gentrified avenue—yet in honor of which the nondescript sky turned quietly pink-toned at dinner time: clumps of space-time in moving contrast to the tan, gray, gridded, rather stupid-looking sharp edges below.

"We lend it [nature] charms that are the reflections of the thoughts in the bottom of our minds, animating and nourishing with our lives the dream which it supplies only with its color."
—Marcel Raymond

Partly.

10/25

The greenish yellow of the ginkgos downstairs against the dun of the building. The *dawn*. No the dun. Dawn would be more interesting.—It's *dun*. Overturned in absentia, pulverized and left to sit out in the flocked atmosphere above Broadway: a horizontal heap, that leaves the orange girder on the sidewalk while deconstructing the roof with (ah!) orange streamers.

—As, for example, the face that got what it deserved at four rather than forty: and is on backwards and has feet for ears.

11/9

"Snow" sky for most of the afternoon after some morning sun. Somewhat dirtier than usual: a herald, or warning, that winter is indeed on its way, presently stacked up somewhere near Jacksonville, Fla.

—At 4:30 PM the gray was lit up by headlights in 2nd, 3rd, 4th and 5th-floor windows.

—4:50: much bluer and (seemingly) purer.

12/1

The backless and halterless immediacy of space

12/4

Les bâtiments de qui je pense que je sais, however the end in sight, if sight is what it is, is both desirable and unrecapturable like a cornerstone formed around a burning coal. The package overturned but not all at once—more the way you pour oat flakes into boiling water. Clearly the apartment buildings are a front for some churning which isn't necessarily a product of thought, though thought is of the essence, leaving the atmosphere alternately sparkling and destitute.

(Earlier.) The first actual snow, lasting about 5 minutes and more like white rain. Yellowish brown backdrop to the east, with black and white slashes through it. Through it all, a few tattered coppery fragments clinging to the few poles that used to be trees on the desert island in the middle of Broadway.

12/20 (2 Christmas cards)
"The south west wind how pleasant in the face"—John Clare

"Basically, artists work out of rather stupid kinds of impulses and then the work is done."—Jasper Johns

8–12/91

141

Urban Landscape
for Ron Padgett

What if
instead of growing
older
we rose,
a few inches
a year, until
approximately
double mature height,
passing every
manner of person
against a background
of windows,
walls, cars, posts
and tree trunks
between the sidewalk
and the second story—
sun
inching down,
clouds strung out overhead.

BUILDING SIXTEENS

[1]
The building is doughnut-colored light
and the colored light behind,
carved shadows included,
is littered with donuts.
            Good spelling doesn't
            get you very far
            in life; nor (counting
            the number of buildings
            which have so far landed)
            are there genuine imperatives
            to go with the structural
            side, the grosser qualities
of things, the ones that settle on
people doing their shopping for them,
planning ornate purposes that glimmer
and delineate before they fade

[2]
as any country's list of principal products
tells a lot about its ways of
thinking about itself and others,
the world of pig-farming humpbacked
            on a horizon on the
            verge of accounting
            to no one, like a blood
            orange teaching its lesson
            to all the other colors,
            particularly at sunset.
            Whence it appears that
            at least since Victorian times,
a troublesome arch has enveloped
people, buildings and landscape
in a fuzzy notion of what it means
to be central, and the stars like brainwaves

[3]
fight through the illusion that we are
command modules illuminated by
some extremely distant source
which gives out, along with throwing
       down its spears, the
       scale which might then be
       noticed and lived in.
       I.e. shooting stars into
       the very idea for the place.
       Just between sentries
       it's cooler, as who would
       burst in oddly continuous
with normal life melting back to
its plinths, brought to the boil
like chicken soup more spun against
than spinning. It isn't after all

[4]
in growing like an apartment building
by cantilevering that humans see
out over their limitations, but a
combination of unrest and purest
       sight, the keenest
       the first to gust as per the day
       and its rather simple-minded
       hours. Improved quarters for
       the pigs, meaning far afield;
       plus some horses silently
       shooting the grays at sunup.
       The quizzed quills found
their way past. (Or as one executed
Elizabethan poet to another, "Dreaming
of many we, excluding they, are awake indeed.")
It implies living for the differentials

[5]
a rash down the sides of row houses
established by the sun that *settles*,
purveyor of order even while the
river driver, askance at all the reroutings,

       casts his gaze towards
       a grove of apple trees, along
       with transplants from
       one friendly star pool.
       To pole through the *un*-
       resolved gallery by
       turns plummeting, a unit
       technically of the upper air

spun of embrace and consignment, each one
on behalf of all its renewals—why is it
upwards of mystical good will bonding
the same guesswork to the dark

[6]
dangerous streets and the ginkgos
forever redeeming them, so that on
reflection they branch out unreflectively
but lifetimes augur weight as well as plumage—
        one consequence of truth
        and its effortless
        lack of consequences,
        spread-eagled, the tresses
        swank in pursuit of the pure dark.
        Let them glaze their wish
        to be air traffic, of a medicinal sort,
        across a sort of carport
into which the nurses who wear their
beauty like the evening rush descend;
excluding some ugly outcroppings of
personal vehicles extended much too far

[7]
witness the armory and all it stands for,
roseness and bigness subtly curved
around news of future occupation
that stunned falls, careless as

       spilling hot coffee. If
       we could take a giant's
       view of an angel settling in
       for another outshining, alone
       of all who spend by virtue
       of that same weather compounded,
       who because the arguable
       stays, come away gracefully

beyond the mere grace of words, the pronoun
and all it knows about not getting caught
on the fire escape as so many things are
in their intent to wave eventually to bubble

[8]
right back to demanding an adjustment
optically and as a kind of translation.
How many mystic wood pheasants would
play Michigan spring beached aplenty,
       an indication that of all
       that has spilled, charm as
       much as unrest squanders
       in the sense of being
       other than what it foreswore,
       all the lofts teetering
       plus all the gulfs surfacing
       out of the normal deep water
—what with scaling down to the deep
romance of debt, typically or not
flooded like an illuminated peristyle, e.g.
the Chinese brother who all unthirsty swallowed

[9]
the sea. Let me not to the true
scattering admit stratagems of watershed
and illusory building outline, whatever
hamfisted buildings pile scraping Oneness

       in an arc that billows

       backwards, as though

       an avenue were a backyard.

       Quiet; you say,

       and no point in keeping clear

       of the citizen in his

       watchful walk through November

       if and only if heel marks

are fatal: if it comes by cargo ship over
the starlight of things which aim upwards
of their outlines, the radii outwards
being the orange or conceivably oblong

[10]
incumbency rising steadily over
the downtown lofts, mingling
inside a system that readily dopes;
of flustered rooftops, radiant lintels,

       factory smoke puffing
       towards its anti-matter
       which gusts honorably if
       conscious of routinely leveraged
       buyouts, handouts making over
       the recompense from *burrowing*
       in the first instance
       and *landing* in the second.
At which point engineering ripples
along the peaks, mounted dry
like valor, if we could pry open the
deficiency.—Careful to be haunted

[11]
in pursuit of the needles which scatter
and blow about on end, not that we need
spiritual references to barge into
when styles change, if they do.

       Use Wortley in a sentence.
       The frog jumped into the
       reflecting pool _____.
       To shift like the future, all
       pulse and fragrance.
       What if we sloped easily, whereas
       we are prevented by such
       conspicuous trifles, only
relatively removed from woodland flowers
that habitually branch out, flame
among corpses of roots and leaves, as though
light green touched with white had spoken out . . .

[12]
effortlessly as provenance, bulked
in chunks and washes . . . odd that they have
even a small secondary imagination
when to get some genuinely public event
       to attach riders remains
       unfloated; while goat,
       donkey, mule, cart
       and lamppost sprinkle the
       distance to burn off, each
       small-town caboose plus
       each receivership whiplashed
       to contrive aureoles out of
the precise relations that don't see to it.
Like pedants (who never get enough *time*
given the celestial curve of their ambition
plus hope plus its meaner suburbs)

[13]

to random field days and above all
decorating along the same detached face,
the star of our self-regard, despite
occasional persons of mixed address
                ending up as musculature
                which is to say stoops
                and reddening sills,
                the public orchestration of
                self-denial taking a leap
                onto the schist below: huddled
                as opposed to the seasonal
                venture that glosses its reprisals
like dentists embroidered onto the same
wallpaper, over and above the fallacy
of the beautiful rippling over people
who ripple into one another like mad

[14]
string beans sunk in the light of their occupied
zenith. A host of boarded up windows
behind which the natural laws keep to
their daily round: black-letter

> and then crystal radio as
> a new troupe makes its
> way out of the cultural quandary
> inordinately abloom,
> proximity to foxgloves
> railroad stations ankle-deep
> even while the city supplies
> keyholes for the asking . . . while

the tributaries supply what we take for granted
in the elevator indicating what people
rise to when they aren't subject to
the grosser play of light and light's failing

[15]
to remain semi-solid, an Aztec sonata
introducing fruit-bearing motifs
to go with the horns. And it attaches
to hair and clothing, thickened
       the way apricots star
       in paint, and it doesn't
       make added sense to say burst
       from the full space between
       in the manner of a keystone,
       yanking and grabbing all
       to the much tuned modern orchestra.
       O that a star sucks up
the low world at random, disinclined to connect,
while their materials pile sky high
at variance with theaters and the pre-war varnish
that irradiates, at variance with alarms

[16]
and let's hope, given the nature of light
and its celestial ambitions that the
time doesn't simply erode, but offers
shoppers the chance to pile into their
        wagons and the row houses
        ahead, evicting above all
        the object-less now that
        some of the foolish ideas have
        been doffed for what they
        are, assemblages whose
        flickerings of life and color
        preclude the ship and its margins.
Forkfuls in shady plots, towed acreage
above all the bars and reflected sunsets,
the chief cup for mailmen here on earth,
decanters filled with wine and express civic virtue.

THE NEARNESS OF THE WAY YOU LOOK TONIGHT

2001

THE PHILOSOPHY OF NEW JERSEY
for Jill

Actually the sky appears older than it is. It's 63 or 64 at most, not 75. The part with the cliff face and the yellow crane could be in its early 30s. It wasn't Wallace Stevens who said, "They have cut off my head, and picked out all the letters of the alphabet—all the vowels and consonants—and brought them out through my ears; and then they want me to write poetry! I can't do it!" It was John Clare. Wallace Stevens said—something like—the best poems are the ones you meant to write. That has a nice sound to it, but it's hard to see how he or anyone would know that. It would be hard, for example, to accept the notion that there are ideas one meant to have. Poems underneath every peeling sycamore and inside every file cabinet, along with ideas about poetry and uncountable other ideas.

THE NEARNESS OF THE WAY YOU LOOK TONIGHT

Smarter than morons are you
Shorter than giants

More reliable than bail-jumpers
Defter than those who are all thumbs

You are nicer than villains
Stabler than those with bipolar illness

Reedier than sousaphones or E-flat horns
More fragrant than monkey houses

Saintlier than mass murderers are you
Peacefuller than janissaries

You are faster than tortoises
Tighter than muumuus

Newer than hand-me-downs
Cleaner than oil & grease stains

Hotter than meat lockers are you
More disinterested than investigative reporters

More heroic than cowards
Healthier than chronic patients

For you are prompter than no-shows
More alive than someone pushing up daisies

Freer than convicts are you
Stronger than weaklings

Svelter than nose tackles
More chivalrous than sentries

You are sprightlier than couch potatoes
More urban than dairy farmers

Rounder than flatworms
Apter than what is irrelevant

Finer than sackcloth are you
Gentler than torturers

Firmer than invertebrates
Kinglier than footmen

Fuller than vacuums are you
More staccato than slurred passages

You are more educable than dropouts
Roomier than crawlspaces

Humbler than showoffs
Closer than the big bang

Wittier than blockheads are you
More legal than after-hours bars

Barer than furnished apartments
Louder than quiet people

CODA: LIGHTER THAN PORTENTS

are you, more reliable than bail-jumpers,
pilloried for having one foot in the air

while the quidditists and eventualists
hole up looking a lot like the September mannerists,
although not as blossoming as the interventionists.

Speaking of bloom, the Chrysler Building equals
everything given away. And the windblown spandrels
unwind the air of pine angels.

CHAIN

Russia is the domed incantation of Kansas
As oceans burn in the individual day.

All day they came and went, sheep dog
Dogged social climber, sedulous

Luster after the Maison d'Infinite
In fine (it looks like) print, the curse of snowflakes.

Lakes abound in western and central Canada.
A part of it has the living tempo

Temporarily slowed, vibrant in
Ranting, the forte of carnations.

Nations become specific groves of ordinariness
Nestled between oceans of stupefaction

Action elbows, like the dark rainbow
Bowing in the new sky, clearing the inevitable

Table piled high with books and reels.
Real spring accumulates: not merely

Leaving the ground but including motion
Shunted previously to space . . .

To a space painted a smooth robin's egg blue.
Bluer than your eyes as you imagine them over the body

Described within this stirred world:
Whirled like letter-writing through a simpler day.

DAY AFTER DAY THE STORM MOUNTED. THEN IT DISMOUNTED

Suppose I am not the uplifter of all I uplift,
in the same sense that the coal-black sky, scumbled and showing a
    few red streaks,
doesn't exactly equal space.

The air is thick. Now it swirls.

It isn't air.

As in the *Iliad*,
death is continually swirling over
the bravest warriors from its source
in some tornado cellar or storage bin of death
and never in a straight line—as though it were embarrassed
to be seen for what it is and chose
the devious route. Not that
it can't directly target those whom it
chooses, but that it chooses not to.

A roughly trapezoidal shadow
has swirled up the side of the building opposite,
making its sooty brick facing darker than normally.
Some cars emerge from its insides.

168

One is making a left turn
from the extreme right lane.

When you think of the
truly instinctual moments, crying out
when the door slams on your foot,
or breathing deeply of spring, it seems only natural
to imagine an opposite way of behaving.

And when instinct is visible,
as clear in the air as leaves and water tanks,
it isn't inconceivable to suppose
an infinite number of possible worlds, bargained for, grasped,
and finally let go at the moment the situation
becomes clear, like storm clouds illuminating a herd of cows
nestled against coal-black tree trunks—*n'est-ce pas?*

And in composing for wind instruments
and putting the same or nearly the same chords
into two different pieces, you are
not likely to hear the same concert at noon
as at dusk—unless, of course, the performances are all illusion
and those in attendance merely marking time
within their own private band shells.

Certo.

An example of feeling
not quite taking the place of thought,
although memorized by it.

The house I live in.
The block of wood and the wood chips,
the surrounding proof that things exist outside the self
despite constant weeding. A waterfall of selves.

The mice are a nice touch, they don't have to speak in complete
    sentences.
Also the sawhorses.
One, sprinkled with life force,
took off a few minutes ago. Stung by its freedom,
whirling to gain a sense of direction,
it hovered over New Jersey for several seconds
before making a U-turn.

No, you turn.

Does the name R. Penis Blavatsky mean anything, at all, to you?

Personally, I think
you need to focus on what is really important to you: change
habits as well as clothes. The shadows
that fall on wet rooftops altering them irrevocably,
new notions in hospital architecture,

half-built buildings with their shirt-sleeved inhabitants
in Italian movies of the sixties, etc.

You, with the neck that moved.
No, *you*; the shadows making their way
inside the paperweight, diffusing the glare that falls on upturned
    palm,
chin, cheek, even the occasional glancing blow
branching off into language.

Here you are a highly educated person. Hands, feet, chin, everything.

One morning, out of the blue,
a flock of wild turkeys
paraded up the hill from the road, at least forty
by actual count. The oddest thing was
their landing on the grass in small squads,
one at a time, with a parent figure
at either end, to march
steadily and without concern
for conceivably life-threatening surroundings
—in sharp contrast to the high-strung and
hyperactive deer—and just as suddenly
vanish into the mix of cedars and dark green shadows.

Here you resemble an aquamanile, your notions poached in rainwater.

Devoted dentist, darling chirurgeon, beloved branch manager,
dear critic, fragrant disciple,
esteemed concert mistress, caring strip miner,
wondrous instantiater, affectionate florist, moving engineer,
imaginative groundskeeper, tender restaurateur,
desirable glazier, charismatic coroner,
self-abnegating occultist, glowing restorer, lissome umpire . . .

Paper-thin traces of Being with needles sticking out of some but
    not all of them . . .

You, for example,
could be the Allegorical Figure of Taxation;
but more (I hope) about that later.

As Dizzy Gillespie is, or was, the god of the winds.

I am at a college interview. Each
of the interviewers is simultaneously
being interviewed. While she fields questions from all sides,
my interviewer shouts questions at me
from the far end of a long refectory table. I can
barely hear her over the din
but find myself admiring the way she responds to
those questions aimed directly at her. Then
I am face to face with someone who
asks if I prefer cloth- or paperbound books; but

just as I am about to respond he takes a wooden spoon
and flings some hard, uncooked grains of oatmeal towards the ceiling
where they hang suspended in the air
like a display of space matter in a planetarium.

Is that lighter—or just grayer?

In fact, for a long time
I've felt like apologizing
for what seem to me excessive references to darkness
as though the available light were on trial.
Sometimes it's virtually impossible
to get up in the morning. The days in
the middle of winter when it doesn't begin
to get light till 7 a.m. or even later,
the swirl commandeering hydrants, curbstones,
stoops, etc. To brush back shadows
from the cheek of night. "To be,"
as Thomas Browne wrote, "a kind of nothing
for a moment," a balloon with a beard . . .

Meanwhile, the cows on the postcard from the college bookstore
have moved from in front of a clump
of shade trees to somewhere more virtual. Peasants
looking stoned, lying face up underneath a table groaning with
    food,
searching the invisible sky as well as each other

for clues regarding their current state: one of
pleasant stupor, or stupefied fullness,
as symbolized in the dazed-looking
small game and surreal life forms attending the postmortem
of what has clearly been a positive experience
for most of them—although not without a trace of some
prior violence, most obviously in long broken cudgels
but also in a branch bent like a catapult
and in the dizzying angle, everything
about to topple into the whirlpool or quicksand of satisfaction
inside which a pipe can tip over a table. (*Das Schlaraffenland*, 1567)

Not exactly pleasant
but not entirely unpleasant either.
Somewhat like "turning
over in your grave." The breeze tingling.

I don't think the subject has changed significantly.

I'm thinking of a noun,
any noun. I picture it
as hard rubber, darkly resinous,
the same family, roughly speaking, as Being-in-Itself.

Each of the slots can be and is filled
by a person, place, thing
or other suitable substantive.

174

Currently the slots come with appropriate hat sizes,
5½ being one of the most popular (Beauty in itself
being rather stupid, in case you haven't already noticed).

While you were painting
the rather severe downpour stopped.
Slowed first, to avoid jolting
the already battered air conditioners.
I don't know about you
but I frequently have the feeling
that the buildings are mere skin, bruised by dusk,
little by little powerless to do
more than ripple, comparable to the rippling that erupts out of
   flatness
to be rolled out and attenuated like the most attenuated
of clouds. What moments are to
themselves: not so much moving as scaffolding.

How do you *know*
or can you *prove*
that the evening doesn't subsist on pure will—
short and fat, thick-necked,
wheezing like a woodchuck, its inner
life a barrel vault, clinging to the last chord played,
the last note written?

In Smokey Joe's Café.

To put it in epic terms—Thinkology
but once removed. How anyone comes to live in
a world of oxbows, steppes, wheat fields, and projective versts.

For you are the electronic type: your keys are oxblood and celadon
    stars.

I see, or am beginning to,
that your reliance on night is genuflectory.
But so do the dark references
resemble life: life after death.
How

it is possible
and also impossible to be the imagination
of a future time. Which is to say that,
given a little more time,
the consequences for both city and rural life
can and must distinguish themselves—unlike the beauties of New
    Hampshire
arm in arm with the beauties of Vermont.

A ball of frosted light
just whirled over the Hudson,
coming to rest on a lamppost. Which
bats it to another. The maroon
of a coffee shop awning utterly divorced from

its lower extenders, barely visible, like the bouffant of an angel

or as Dorothy Wordsworth reported
of an especially beautiful May afternoon, "I drank
a little Brandy and water, and was in heaven."

Clearly not the same as
landing in the middle of Herald Square
wearing Valkyrie gear and dancing a pavane
to celebrate the sudden change in seasons.

Still,
comparison to the other arts seems
all but inevitable, as witness the so-called
Clarinetist's Fallacy, coaxing excessive
feeling out of what is essentially a cold instrument
if brilliantly so—the result being a whining
masquerading as feeling

whereas the best playing is "cold and passionate
as the dawn."

"The reed is held on the mouthpiece
by a soft rubber support which has sluts.
A very pure dound is obstained by an metallic plate
mounled directly behind of the rubber support.
The whole device is in the form of a flexible band very resistant

adjusted by two screws, to allow adjustment for personal playing styles . . .

    —casy sound production
    —a very rich sounding note
    —a naturally obstained pure sound.

        A/Remove the adjusting screurs
        B/Place the reed on the mathpiece
        C/Carefully position the ligature around the mountpiece plus
            reed
        D/Fit the crews and tighten . . ."   [sic]

Foghorns in the atmosphere
of Smokey Joe's Café. In
or just behind it, in an alleyway
lined with stucco and graffiti from the sixties.

As the life force plays tricks
plus the two Brahms sonatas for clarinet (or viola) and piano.

Some whiteness is beginning
to show around the edges
but not in all places at once.
The bills have been paid; Mozart
is playing quietly in the background
aged 2½; a few of the dark clumps, wads of emptiness,
anchor the deer and the echoing cedars. A few

more particles than usual: to put aside, focus on, or just
chuck out never and nowhere to be witnessed again ever.

Your lids are getting heavy.
People carrying water faucets keep attempting to put you out.

North of the Charles . . .

My name,
actually my middle name, is Alphonse
and I live in northern Alberta,
but have a summer palace near Albuquerque.
Of adobe. Behind the brickwork.

The close colors depart in droves.

To write
                    a nation or thriving city-state.
The Queen Anne's Lace
                                        dove in.

Meanwhile, deer consumption
—by and not of—
has proceeded at a fairly alarming rate.
Nearing the surface they chin upwards
slicing the air into deer and not-deer. Pruning
to within an inch of life, which in this case

happens to read as broad daylight
despite a charcoal gray fuzz directly overhead
like a sweater on a minaret.

You have received a grant to do hornet work . . .
standing on your head
not to mention endless attention to the shivers
that erupt. There was a just stained look to the sky
that lasted most of the morning, leaving
rags at the edges. Not merely cloud shreds
or broccoli-covered cliffs; the perforations
through which the breeze enters like woodwinds: the bright glow
        of new leaves
magnetizing unspeakably charged states of being.

Just before dusk,
a whole notebookful of sense impressions flitted around
the trunk of a maple tree,
a fairly young one,
looking for a hole in the protective wrapping.

A woman in a cream-colored blouse and blue apron
bends at a 90° angle to fill a lustrous pitcher from a
        copper-colored urn.
Leaning out the window the evening clouds floated by.

STUDY FOR "DAY AFTER DAY THE STORM MOUNTED. THEN IT DISMOUNTED"

Devoted dentist, darling chirurgeon, beloved mailman,
dear critic, fragrant disciple,
esteemed second violinist, caring strip miner,
delightful bagman, wondrous instantiater,
affectionate florist, moving engineer, embraceable barber,
imaginative umpire, tender restaurateur,
desirable glazier, lissome dwarf, humble go-getter,
self-abnegating groundskeeper, glowing restorer, tender agent,
ravishing dunner, adored kayaker,
considerate bathing beauty, warm slam-dunker, delicate rabbi,
undisgruntled grant applier, tasteful chastiser,
huggable frontier scout, kind futurist, lively thief,
haunting numismatist, glistening bartender,
full-breasted chairperson, melting dealer, translucent branch
    manager,
angelic burgomaster, generous do-it-yourselfer,
herniating operatic tenor, congenial wide receiver,
exemplary bailiff, stimulating mobster, cute rumrunner,
willowy executionist, life-promoting tour guide,
handy antagonist, caressed misprizer,
cherished inkeeper, head-turning pharmacist,
ached-for sous chef, unforgettable fogie, seductive pointillist,
riveting sophist, missed beadle, magnetic muezzin,

well-meaning bowler, dedicated phrenologist,
precious typist, seraphic song stylist, winsome CEO,
idolized quick study, dearly beloved test pilot,
undetested laundress, pet decoder, lovesome party leader

PHILOSOPHICAL SONGS

1. Some of Them That Do Fish Will Go for A Midnight Swim

It's not so much the partis pris as
the performance which is then called into question.
Then back to the dents. Embrace of atmosphere

which isn't the wind that collects on the windowpane,
the word skidding dispassionately by way of
your gown of powder blue light. The cedars slip.

2. As Moonlight Becomes You

refining the swale for the sake of
ordinary life, which isn't orderly
but does undergo a pattern of resolute change
because you supply the necessity: hence

ordinary life which isn't orderly,
marches on ahead into a swirl of reddening leaves
because you supply the necessity. Hence
the moon is rampant, flitting between you.

3. Madrigal

Not border or pass—not quite
        past either, post? postern? as
in the past reaching around its
turquoise plinth despite a coating of melted pine needles
or are they melting meanwhile the landscape has turned
        arrow-like to waste.

Distant squawks and pained foothills
not painted, not *intricately*
personal at best. Yet a morsel
off the top of a silo, flung from a train
closer than phenomenology more rapid than song.

Words from Robert W. Service

The things you had no right to do, the things you should have
    done,
Of cities leaping to stature, of fame like a flag unfurled
And a city all a-smoulder and . . . as if it really mattered.
And the greasy smoke in an inky cloak went streaking down
    the sky.

It sort of made me think a bit, that story that you told
All glamour, grace and witchery, all passion verve and glow,
The all-but-fluid silence,—yet the longing grows and grows.
Now wouldn't you expect to find a man an awful crank!

For the debit side's increasing in a most alarming way
From the vastitudes where the world protrudes through clouds
    like seas up-shoaled.
So the stranger stumbles across the room, and flops down there
    like a fool
Dreaming alone of a people, dreaming alone of a day.

The Wanderlust has haled me from the morris chairs of ease
By the darkness that just drowns you, by the wail of home desire.
It's also true I longed for you and wrote it on an egg . . .
Though where I don't exactly know, and don't precisely care.

It seems it's been since the beginning; it seems it will be to the end
To hit the high spots sometimes, and to let your chances slip.
For the lake is yonder dreaming, and my cabin's on the shore.
In the little Crimson Manual it's written plain and clear:

We're merely "Undesirables," artistic more or less,
The people ever children, and the heavens ever blue,
Dear ladies, if I saw you now I'd turn away my face
Oh, the clammy brow of anguish! the livid, foam-flecked lips!

I'm not so wise as the lawyer guys, but strictly between us two
I'm the Steinway of strange mischief. We're all brutes more or less.
Then you've a hunch what the music meant . . . hunger and
    night and the stars.
All honey-combed, the river ice was rotting down below.

LINES

Technically unwinding its purchase power
despite the roofs and their allover blind,
pronouncing an effect of vines

bearing grapes at intervals backwards
to the mostly distressed values,
private interest coterminous with public leaching out

to enlist the mobile freedoms,
of increased expectancy including but not confined
to putting the numbers in line,

while the slick streets are being swept
by all the emotional legwork to be done,
who and what final wrangling with the gap

between sure deadline and unsecured future
captioned in irises, while the qualifiers
push on ahead, any organ defined or implied by work

that hits home at the first pragmatics,
threatening a wheat field or sudden burst of spring
dripping color along a riveted earth.

NOTE ON FOG

I like Augustine's calling lust a "fog." Of course he didn't say it
in English and didn't call it embarrassing. I also like the image
of the critic who wouldn't know a poem if it came up and bit
him. I picture him, or her, not necessarily an evil person, having
finished some minor chore like taking out the garbage, when
this *thing* strikes. The fog of surprise and not, at least relatively
speaking, the blood or teeth marks. The utter disorientation,
seeing things and not seeing anything.

Disrobing (On the Same Theme)

wearing a robe, and then getting rid of it. The French *enrobé*, meaning so thick it has to be licked off. Last night was robed in a thick, grainy fog that dissipated late this morning. Even so, the air isn't quite itself, shielded from its deepest concerns—and from a few superficial ones as well. In my judgement, or judge-a-ment as former President Gerald Ford used to pronounce it, echoing the traditional tripartite division of mental faculties, it's going to clear up, but probably not before the middle of the afternoon. Also in the judge-a-ment of the local TV forecaster. What moral philosophers since Plato have deemed judge-a-ment as powerful as will ("the strongest oaths" being "straw to the fire i' the blood"), i.e., serious rivals for moral attention? Sometimes what appears to be judge-a-ment is robed in sleep, or something resembling it. A grainy fog casting everything in a gray blur. Then someone named Moriarty steps out of the grain, his thought processes enrobed in mystery, shedding fog in spangles of black-and-white.

ATTRIBUTES OF POETRY
for Marjorie Welish

1

The Floridas of the soul
Not the mental Floridas the Floridas that happen to brush by
    on the street wearing musk and little else

2

For the sun goes down its hairline studded with cumquats

3

One of several fissures like reading aloud to a horse
What of the head the head is lost in thought

4

What of the feet navigating through quicksand not necessarily
    of their own choosing
What of the little world of the eye

5

Circumscribed
That people had brains at least until quite recently

6

Use pectin in a sentence
They were pectin like sardines
The robins pectin the trees all day and all night

7

He pectin a terrible hurry

8

Nicer than villains taller than inchworms faster than slowpokes
More opaque than Philip Johnson's Glass House

9

Striding towards Eleusinian life have you noticed how much
    detail goes into paralleling the flow of earth
The last two summers were in fact quite nice

10

If not an angel in a business suit then diopters of space and time
Attractive deer with on-site experience seeks new orientation
    the darker and more galluptious the better

11

The slipcase for a few minor league stars

12

Taking courses

Where one course ends and another course begins

What it means to be a course (what it would be *like* to be a
course)

13

History minus the stopping equaling a kind of prehistory

Or medium in which it is possible to frame units of pre-judgement

14

A kind of solid space with feathers sticking out

TRIO FROM WANG WEI
for Larry Fagin

1. Mullion Hotel

The roof raises its music stand at ease.
Dormers unscrolling their window boxes.
Kick the confusion along the ramp, through the antennae!
To presage you while your plié breaks out in morning glories.

2. Lightness Eye

The gong shampoos the January rain.
Then, when you are rendered like song,
Fence-sitting (lying—) like Russian linen,
Foo! Show the king the tea of shame!

3. Character AS Character

The hills are bare you can't make out anyone,
Still as sounds form persons the air is all conversation,
The forest of sunset licks its way inward.
Above the north-facing moss the sky is green, black—and
    blue!—ribbon.

Initial N

Artifice,
Fistulous

Luster,
Tergiversation

Shunning machinery
Re storms and

Sand-like oriels.
All reels

(Ils attendent)
A tendency

Seeded with
Withholdings.

Inks deafened
Indoors

Or seized evidence:
A dense star

Starring Diderots,
Roses to summon

Monsters,
Ersatz eyes.

I sing the ginkgos
Cozy (human—) as

Asterisks,
Risks inside art.

Landscape & Chardin
for Trevor Winkfield

I have to confess that *Bon appétit* never strikes me as an appropriate invitation. It seems too...medicinal, like charging a poem with the obligation to improve, or at least define, one's sense of self. Speaking of which, how many of our great poets are themselves more than 8% of the time? Not just the obvious cases. Take Yeats. Or take Hart Crane. Take almost anyone. I don't feel as confident saying so, but I'm pretty sure the same is true for painters even if the percentages go up some. So much of what we experience as present is earmarked for the future. Sing, Contingency, of a single membrane in the process of becoming a frame house open to the charcoal and cantaloupe of evening— of the unfavored nation status of line. I like the idea that the air is too close to either prove or disprove its existence, and that it has no stake whatever in the issue. The deer are practically pets. A few days ago, the small one that lay down to die got up when no one was looking. No one ever sees a live skunk, yet we take the facts of its life on the evidence. Along with a certain amount of shivering and pure, or at least uncharacterizable, *qualia*. The impressions planted before the realms collide. Still, the houses, linear or not, retain a humanity despite their continuity with anything and everything, power and phone lines as much as faraway loosestrife whose color (whatever else it may take cover under) floods the eye. The pond calmed down earlier. Written on in only a few spots apart from the questionable egrets—living question marks is what I mean. I don't, personally, see much suffering other than the everpresent kind. I can envision the Incredible Shrinking Man, by now not so incredible, up to his neck in ground cover or the dried up stalks showing above the pond surface, barely taking in the postings against deer-hunting, the freeze-frames of the hawks, the occasional ghostly flock of wild turkeys among the ubiquitous cedars—plus hints of yet-to-be-instantiated structure. The lintels, what there is of them, are heartbreaking.

Typing and Typing in the Wandering Countryside

including the pond bitten down to its cuticles,
whatever you were doing pursuant to flatness

it doesn't mean we exist as writing.
What is flat is on trial for its flatness.
Whatever you were doing pursuant to flatness

is a particular: it is its own witness.
While air billows and closes around the petal of evening

(whatever you were doing pursuant to flatness)
it doesn't mean we exist as writing
— fringed in charcoal and umber fields, loosestrife utterly
   mismanaged.

CADENZA

2007

CADENZA

The longer the life
the roomier the harbor.

Well, not exactly ...

Partly though. The sails
continuous with the furled and expectant moments
making their sum bad writing (when they write at all).

Yesterday about 10 a.m. Hopkins stopped by. He seemed absorbed.
This morning: gray, rainy, somewhat anxious, eager for the landscape
to proceed ... you go first; no,
you. Suppose I hold the door for you.
Thank you; but *no*.

This is a hunch, but I'll bet
even the Medusa, grim as she was, took a shower
at least once in a while,
tossing her "hair" around until it dried
if not exactly shone—not that anyone could live to tell the tale
or for that matter distinguish between things suddenly petrified
and rock-laden Greece.

Lately, for some reason,

I've grown quite interested in small start-up businesses.
Particularly the choice of locations.
The fact that so many start-ups fail
(whether due to vagaries of economic climate, misreading of
    neighborhoods
—which I personally believe isn't given sufficient
credit as an explanation—or just plain mismanagement)
doesn't seem to diminish their number
let alone the poignancy inherent in ribbon-cutting.

A recent example: one seemingly choice location
almost directly across the street
went begging for an entire year. Finally,
an espresso bar opened—only to close within six months;
followed by a branch of an outfit specializing
in low-cost back massage; and now (already there are signs of
    imminent failure)
a branch of a discount shoe store chain.

In response to your recent enclosure, let me say initially
that it's o.k., you don't *have* to change anything—though I would
at least think about "continuous" preceding "as the stars that shine."
It's not that the analogy isn't evocative; but is that
really what starlight looks like
to the naked eye? (continual? contiguous? which would have to be
in the extremely rare temporal sense
bringing risks of its own, which I'm not sure you want to risk

since when all is said and done the last thing you want to do
is stop your reader!). I'm not,
by the way, hinting that everything has to be absolutely
clear or reasonable, visually or in any other way. Have you thought
about trying it as a pantoum, or a sestina?

It must be true, mustn't it
that the more ideas you have
and are able to express in some intelligible form to others
the fuller life is for all concerned—notwithstanding
the perfectly natural fear
that the ideas you do have,
for all the fireworks of the night before,
can and frequently do appear wan and even sheepish
in morning sunlight.

"Thinking on paper"
is one aspect. Another is
the ghostly traces of mind that hover
over whatever is in the process of being constructed,
whether lyric poem or midtown office building.
"Ghostly" because the connections between
mind and world are invariably impossible to make out,
not to speak of the "rewriting aspect" seemingly built
into the nature of things.

One of the more disturbing ideas, at least in my view,
is that all thinking entails something like
"triage" among competing ideas,
such that the contents of mind
at any given moment aren't,
and can't be, an accurate representation
of the mental processes involved—and moreover,
that they mask equally significant mental activity
which hasn't (for reasons
that are plainly unavailable)
been selected, but which could equally have been so,
given even minuscule variation in our complex mental life.

But this is the point at which the portable typewriter (I still
use one of the old manual ones)
went on the fritz, inconveniently or not;
and I didn't feel like paying more
to have it repaired than I paid for it originally!
Plus the reconditioning fee I always seem
to get talked into. The Frank Gehry buildings really did move;
but the reality in that case was the dream.
Still, the dream involved ideas.

"Baseballically speaking,"
as former Red Sox slugger Ted Williams
once began a response to a TV interviewer,
it's as though the outfield fences have been moved in,

leaving less room to maneuver
but *a fortiori* more opportunity for transcendence.
Nonetheless, the gaps (late afternoon shadows in clumps) remain
    poignant,
like those "queasy 'being' emotions which,"
according to the philosopher Roger Scruton
whom some are inclined to write off as a conservative
(and worse), "lead to drink and metaphysics."

The shadows twist the argument "like we did last summer."

How about stopping with the syllepses—or Whitman!

Clearly, I don't seem to be able to . . . at least it's taking a lot more
    time
than I expected.
As for the day as a whole, it came and went,
I think it's fair to say,
minus any notable losses, notwithstanding
the fragment of cornice that broke off
the roof of a pre-war apartment building, grazing
a dark green Subaru wagon parked below
but fortunately no passers-by. What Thoreau,
the Thoreau, was doing poking around the construction site
for the new neighborhood Arts Theater
I haven't a clue, any more than I know
what was in the brown paper bag his mother (it certainly appeared
    to be)

brought him at approximately noon. Sky earlier not quite angry
as in an "angry throat," but definitely annoyed.
The city trees, the sycamores, acacias, Callery pears, lindens and
    ginkgos,
were all waving their arms, clearly delighted to be doing so,
but it is the ginkgos whose humanity continues to be born anew.

Speaking of which, some believe that as a result
of the current recycling craze
which it certainly is, the very notion of *new*
is acquiring a negative connotation such as *plastic* once had
and retains in those areas
where traditional materials such as metal and wood
have demonstrated themselves to be elegant as well as durable,
e.g., certain high-end SLR cameras and a few extant
makes of manual portable typewriters; although
here, too, it must be said that quality is more and more being
sacrificed on the altar of the brand name gods.

A few light drops have begun falling
close to where the twenty-foot-long, late 50s
mauve Cadillac with the For Sale sticker
was parked seemingly forever, without,
amazingly, being towed or stripped for parts
or otherwise interfered with. At one point light appeared
to shoot out from its fins in reddish squalls
reminiscent of some of Philip Guston's abstract paintings from
    the 50s.

And the evening, already fully loaded, drops
into its pumice sea.

North to Reznikoff. The storm
struck as forecast, tearing big branches loose from their moorings,
leaving mature evergreens maimed, bloodied,
in advanced stages of syphilis, diabetes, and osteoporosis,
leaving (for some few minutes afterwards)
a thin wash of blue sky
like the melody that breaks in fleetingly
in the second movement of Chopin's Second Sonata.
Has there been a literary critical backlash,
beginning at the basketball pole
and continuing all the way to the Catskills?

Then I am at the bottom
of an extremely tall, vaguely cylindrical
(something about it reminds me of a free-form glass candy bowl)
swimming pool which has the water painted up the sides
and no clear point of exit or entry.
Far off, near what must be the top, is what looks like
a porthole where, if the pool were in fact filled,
a swimmer could theoretically exit—although
if this were as well the point at which
the water entered, exiting would be problematic to say the least.
The water is painted in a pleasing
—actually dry-looking—powder blue,

more the look and feel of sky than water,
neither realistic nor stylized (in the manner,
say, of a Hokusai) but somewhere between the two.
The English painter David Hockney, who has in fact
painted swimming pools, comes to mind.

All viewpoints coexist, if not
at precisely the same moment
then within the same spatial/temporal frame,
the tragic, so-called, barely pulled back down
onto its stone bench and efforts to
disentangle tragic from comic outlooks
doomed to wrong-headedness if not out-and-out failure.
Like, I have to say, the widow of the English poet and courtier
Sir Walter Ralegh, who kept her dead husband's head
for weeks beside her bed in a red leather bag. As John Sloan said,
"It makes living, living. It makes starving,
living." Numerous persons, many out of focus,
rush in and out of a rural train station carrying all their belongings,
stowing them above and underneath their seats,
taking them out again and staggering down platform steps
before doing an about-face, while a Sousa march,
The Thunderer, blares from the station's multiple loudspeakers.
It's not that we say (or ever would),
"It's a red leather day," but that
Screwball Tragedy, so-called,
is never far off the mark. Take the names. Take Ajax

and Jocasta and Medea.

Please.

I fall upon the books of life, I read.

—Me too. But I find it useful,
at least some of the time, to think in a focused manner
about the writing process,
the "ghost" directing the machine. One thing
I've found that doesn't help
is the word-processing programs that think
they know what it is you're about to write
before you do and fill in the blanks,
and frequently if not invariably get it wrong
and think you're writing a report to shareholders
when you're smack in the middle of your film script or Spenserian
    sonnet.

Then someone stirs
in the next room and it is as though the roof fell in,
as far as the writing is concerned.

(Then it's simply too dark to write without a flashlight,
which I don't have—although, truth to tell, this was the point
at which the only pencil I had with me broke and, dumb me! I had
completely forgotten to bring along a sharpener

let alone a backup. Eventually finding a local shopkeeper,
a butcher who happened to be open late for business,
I inquired whether he had anything sharp
I could borrow just for a moment. In response,
he sang a few bars of "How High the Moon"
and proved himself prophetic. "Not that sharp!"
we all chimed in, good-naturedly. But I had to miss parts of a late
"down" afternoon, plus early evening, of recording.)

Why shouldn't
Athena's famously gray eyes further
signify human limitation, even fundamental lack,
as in our modern notion of "gray areas,"
the limitations built in if often (fortunately) obscured.

The following are congratulated for obtaining their degrees
and instructed to return caps and gowns
(as well as overdue library books) to avoid fines: James Anthony
    Pinto,
Marilhou Aubry, Philip Kwan, Margarita Komarovsky,
Simonne Pollini, Igor Oytser, Soraya Hazrat Sayeed,
Melissa C. Schouls, Sean S. Samad, Christiana Sciaudone,
Charles Alexander Mujahes, Shirley I. Robinson,
Anna Lisa Bella, Darline Lalanne, Marcia P. Turk,
Motoko Miyama, Joseph C. Scorcia, Rose-Elizabeth DePasquale,
John D. Drinkman, Jr., Amanda Jill Bernstein,

Christopher Edward Quirk, Candida Lynn Tapia, Brian Elmer
    Taylor,
Richard Edward Heater, Melisa Ng, and Ronnie Cummings; with
apologies to any whose names have been misspelled or
unintentionally omitted. Naturally, those who own
their caps and gowns (or who have received written extensions
from the library) are excluded. Be sure the writing is legible.

In a crowded off-Broadway theater,
a heckler refuses to sit down despite mounting threats
from the relatively large audience. Several of the costumed and in
    some cases masked actors
(they are doing Shakespeare's *A Midsummer Night's Dream* in
    traditional dress)
though visibly distracted, climb down from the stage
and form a protective ring around him. Bottom
appears to be the ringleader.

How About Stopping with the Syllepses—or Whitman!
for Ed Barrett

Chalk it up to November or the third base coaching box . . .

Just when it twisted the argument "like we did last summer,"
it creeps past its logical conclusion towards the HOV lane.
It's like being named to the Commission, or McProblem-Solver.
You skip a beat then the two most difficult analogies
leaving a scooped-out feeling, the bases empty with two out in
    the ninth
and the clarinet solo climbing on its own in the *Seventh.*

Romantic Note

Pieces—stems, ghosts—of afternoon
falling all over themselves
into evening—the doughty Queen Anne's lace
threatening to leave its bed
so "order growing from rank disorder" is a dream if not
a simple category mistake, with
or without your tacit consent
you want particulars I'll show you
particulars see here they are
I hold them towards you

SONNET

The tone poem left the door open.
Well, *close* it.
It doesn't stay. It reminds me of
Elizabethan plays where eyes,
especially the tragically blinded ones, are "jelly."
It has a center with a circumference loosely attached.
The ideas about social wastefulness
smeared over individual needs.

Since the ideas about wastefulness
are smeared over their objects,
the tone is everywhere.
It expresses its reluctance as virtue.
It is reluctant to intrude, like minds into
the fleetingness they concede.

BOUL' MICH
for Walter Srebnick

You're in print about the connections between
poetry and bowling. Perhaps you'd like to comment further
on what you once characterized as "strikes, spares, splits
and the heartbreak of the gutter ball." It was the Boul' Mich,
wasn't it, where you spent so much time as an 11- and 12-year-old?
I always thought that was a clever name for a bowling alley.

—Are you sure you're not referring to the time
I was talking about poetry and *bowing*? [laughs] Arco,
pizzicato, sostenuto, playing with all 13 strings, or however many
there are? [laughs] Come to think of it,
the *Boeing* idea isn't so bad either, flying away on the "viewless
     wings
of poesy." I'll leave the ailerons and Fasten Your Seatbelts signs to
     you. [laughs]

Was it the classic 7-10 or some other split you once compared to
John Donne's "stiff twin compasses"? Was that meant
to be taken seriously, rather than as one of your well known
     witticisms?

—Do bowling alleys sell beer? [laughs]

So I gather that you continue to find the conceit meaningful,
    which is to say
illuminating in terms of poetry.

—Obstacles crop up. Sometimes you knock them over
sometimes not. By the way, it was the Bowl Mitch,
the alley belonged to a guy named Mitch. I probably gave it a
    French "twist"
during one of the interviews you're probably remembering
—without remembering. [laughs]
Everything gets toted up on the overhead scoreboard.

So if I understand correctly, you have a setup
which corresponds to a poem's premise,
followed by a dynamic, which on the bowling side involves a
    certain number of steps,
release of the ball, roll down the alley, and contact—or not. Does
    that
parallel inspiration, drafts, and finished poems? Might it apply
in a structural sense to the opening lines, body, and conclusion
of a particular poem? What happens if you tear up a poem
midway in the process, just throw it in the basket?

—If I call a way of doing something "pizzicato"
rather than "arco," does that necessarily imply that I'm using
a pencil and a notebook rather than a word processor? [laughs]

Maybe it's time we took a break. One of the things
I want to be sure to follow up on is your remark long ago
about empty lanes, and whether that was prompted by Robert
    Frost's famous analogy
between free verse and playing tennis without a net.

—Or a full deck. [laughs] By the way,
empty lanes are beautiful in themselves . . . the sheen of the wood,
patterns of inlays, contrasts between adjoining lanes and gutters . . .
    wouldn't you
agree that wood, like words themselves, has its own beauty?

Of course.

—And the ball rolling down the polished surface has
what might be called an "animated" or "kinetic" beauty?

Yes, now that you mention it.

—Isn't it also true that the beauty of collision
is something quite different from the beauty of evasion
or the beauty of tabulation?

Do you have the impression that others—critics, academicians,
    other poets—
go along with your schema? I mean, I've never heard the connection
made elsewhere. Have you gotten any feedback over the years,

positive or negative?

—What do you think? [laughs]

I probably should know this, but have you written any poems
in the shape of bowling balls or bowling pins?

—You mean with finger holes? [laughs]
I have an early one based on the 7–10 split you mentioned earlier.
The law of the excluded middle. [laughs]

We've now had our third pot of freshly brewed espresso
and practically finished a delicious white chocolate mousse
with key lime flavoring. The cedar trees outside the window
are virtually black. I have the strong sense of a writer
confident both in his abilities and in his unique perspectives,
no matter how unusual they may appear to others. Whereas,
at first glance, the poetry-bowling connection (similarly, if
not so elaborated, the poetry-bowing and poetry-Boeing
        connections)
may seem a thin enough conceit, the more entertained
as they say, the more eloquent, as the bayberry candle on the
        kitchen table
lends a glow to the vegetable patterns on the window curtains
which wouldn't have seemed possible earlier. I'm increasingly
        aware of
the fragile fortifications between dusk and evening, as though

the former had been erected only for the latter to knock it
down. . . .Have you
ever written what, in your mind, is a 300 poem?

—Piece of cake. [laughs] Crash! [laughs]

THREE ON A MATCH

Shine nakedly
—Wallace Stevens

Don't be a Dutch door or 6-hour calls to the heart of Lapland

Down the sides of the museum forming a threadbare port

Be not angst among the angels

I don't ever think I shall see it elasticized

Don't be a duck on ice-skates or a tomato

Your address has been lost please send a brand new one not a
    made-up one

Not the bust of a sea monster on a scumbled brown stone shelf

Not a cup on a willow tree or the signpost between Mudvilles

VETOED

like to the curious builder
—Paul Violi/Samuel Daniel

1. Winter Palace/Ski Lodge

Not, as it looks from close up, a snowmobile constructed of ice slabs and rock salt, rather all styrofoam in the shape of a cup lying on its side. Flagstone stained light brown, heated from underneath for the steam and the spills—apart from this no reference to winter. The atmosphere, equally hot and cold, permeated by a fragrance that produces instantaneous alertness and a desire to smoke, regardless of fear of death and/or chronic illness.

2. Mausoleum for a C.E.O.

A large, graceful—pianist's, say, Horowitz's—hand with five gradually ascending entrance ramps leading to a vaulted interior. The vaulting can be rib or fan so long as there is space for small skylighting at the "knuckles." At the very back (black-and-white view of pine woods laden with snow) a rough, dimly lit wall of stucco or poorly aligned brick painted to look like a hacked-off wrist. Music permanently piped in, all Chopin, preludes, nocturnes, etudes, mazurkas, waltzes, scherzos, sonatas, impromptus, Polonaises, ballades.

3. Factory Town Ballpark

AM radio, on exceptionally high stilts like the huts in *Outcast of the Islands*. Fifties console style, or at the least lacking any reference to high tech—especially not black. Gates, ramps, booths, entrances, "skyviews," etc., sealed up.—Or else a press box "open unto the fields, and to the sky," which is brilliant October blue at the dome and only slightly withered at the rim, dropping off into grimy pendentives.

4. Urban Sheepfold

Sweaters, socks, collars, seat covers, linings, whatever—so long as it is all light beige or dirty cream and the texture contrasts with the flat planes of city reality. On the inside walls pornographic murals are an option. A hint—without overstating it—of blood outside would be useful, as would a large grindstone, which could be placed in a courtyard in back, visible when both front and garden doors are open or "disguised" as a dish antenna on the roof, silicates catching the sun and shattering it into grit and crystals all over the sidewalk.

5. Architectural Firm

Paperwork and more paperwork. Unbuilt projects—sketches, drafts, contracts and so on—piled higher than the Empire State Building against a blue sky dotted with artificially white clouds that catch up the various whites of the paper. Some but not all of the projects have legible writing; which ones and how many (as opposed to those whose verbal element is merely suggested, as in certain painterly paintings) are optional, e.g., Poet's Fireplace, Palace of Theory, Art and Philosophy Majors Union, Pan-Racial Dome, High Renaissance Elevator, Dugout after Géricault, Left Bank Cinema, Institutional Bike Rack, ATM Group, Rooftop Water Tanks for Upper West Side Skyline, EST Center, Suburban Think Tank, Feathered Tower for Bird Sanctuary, Band Shell for the Hudson Near Catskill, N.Y., Gang Headquarters, Protected Salt Lick, Taxi & Limousine Pergola, Tick-Free Habitat, Hole-in-the-Wall Temple, Plan for Utilization of Castle Duct and Crawl Space, Studio for a Realist Painter, William Tell Monument for East Approach to Brooklyn Bridge, Portable Tailor's Nook, Boccie Field Grandstand, Baroque Environment, Vertical Subway Station, Four-Poster Conference Table for Heads of State After the Bed of Ware, Buoyant Bridge, Globe Theater, Courtyard for a Maximum Security Prison, Postal Workers Lounge, Outdoor Bowling Alley, Skateboard Space Patterned After Chinese Scroll, Hospice Combining the Well with the Sick, Communal Swing, Subtly Graduated Chimneys, Spandrels for a Court Building, Locks for a Small Canal, West-

Facing Stringcourse, Rose Window for a Motel, Dental Office Entrance, Art Deco Barracks, Tropical Washroom, Insurance Office Atop Statue of Atlas Holding Up the World, Monument to Lust, Hotel Foyer with Ice Statue of Epimetheus, Ebbets Field Memorial, Coffered Ceiling for Stock Exchange, Double Monument to Vermeer and Chardin, Computer Dating Lounge, Balusters for Teller's Line after Robert Adam, Pulpitum for Quarantining, Prep School Gargoyles, Victory Arch for Arbitrage Firm Headquarters, Sketch for Ceiling Garden, Out-of-Scale Staircase, Bridge Covered in Satin, Ornamental Cave, Old-Style Record Store on Revolving Plinth, New Jersey Wetlands Villa Rotonda, Subterranean Office for a Bookie, Garden Restaurant Cornice with Solar Panels, Desert Island Bungalow, Dormer with Built-in Antenna, Rackstraw Downes Commemorative Frieze for Dragon Cement Factory, Bar for Intellectuals, Herbal Tea Parlor, Glass Hovel, Monument to City Winter in the Shape of a Bus Piled High with Snow, Men's Room Quincunx, Roller Derby Arena in the Form of a Cyclotron, Row Houses Catching Late Sun.

STUDY

It must be daylight
Your painting of chicory dividing a dark green field
Fills on all sides with light.
It must be daylight.

Some of the portions which are out of sight
Become what the painting yields.
It must be daylight:
Your painting of chicory dividing a dark green field.

HOLY SONNET

1

Do something like the eyebrow colonials
coming into their own.

2

The chrome of the new, carefully
wiped down to exclude hangers-on (it looks like but
it isn't the case that the worst is past, from
a healthy enough interest in being
to an almost pathological distrust of non-being)
who do the smearing.

3

At such times the dander moves over. A hole in a building
could be a verb as well as an office romance.
Move the speck. It doesn't have to be
a Baltimore oriole, bursting and blooming.

CLIP FROM FRANCIS JAMMES

There would be wasps and roses all over.
Late afternoon bells. Grapes transparent as stones
asleep in sun and warm shadow.
I would love you there!
I give you my heart, every ventricle,
and my brittle spirit, half secret pride
half the white roses of my own poems.
And still I can't make you come to life!
I'm positive that by now we would be kissing and more,
adrift on the grass near a cool stream.
Shadows piled on all the leaves.
What I said about noise: the burning sun.
Shadows: from the hazel trees.
The taste on your lips (mixed) white grapes,
wasps, red roses.

OCTOBER

Slipping its height as per the aspirin of
your fullest sleep, the perennial spine.

O the angels of arrant tempo fold
graves for the brandishing, under the gravity

misnaming looks—as well as avid and filled
to print away honey on what abandoned.

What is bought when the wing is handed
over to georgics, less the cortex that rides

roughshod over heather, money down at the docks
heaving its shadows more or less openly

patrolling the outer limits of inspection,
reverent as decoys? To magnify the vessel while it

splits into almond blossoms, a stupid
statesman; and visibly shaken, and note how others

are the first to throw chairs around the room
countenanced by the verge of the light

fielding October, with possible annexation of the grocery stores, brandy bottles floating to their ultimate lays.

MY SHIP HAS SAILS
(after Hafiz)

Some poets are prose-poets digitally remastered as poets

Others ruin their daily lives nor does thy beauty show itself
   unless
someone is there to harvest it, in pumpkin lamplight

Yet you NORTH standing on your head
and playing the Selmer alto, the fragment of a sail

Each time you think the scaffolding is complete
her name hits the awning and gold stripes all along Broadway

TRANSLATION

I feel you very close to me
In the same way that sky and air seem not two things but one
Those termite-like pests are attacking the two-by-fours
O two-by-fours

In the same way that sky and air seem not two things but one
The small elevations eventually touch
O two-by-fours
Masked like cattle with cutouts of sun glued to them

The small elevations eventually touch
All they are allotted in the way of dull urban skies
Masked like cattle with cutouts of sun glued to them
To make a long story short we need extricating

All they are allotted in the way of dull urban skies
The streams on the map lend something of themselves
To make a long story short we need extricating
Though that doesn't hold a candle to out-and-out mental disarray

The streams on the map lend something of themselves
Periodically rising above the longing
Though that doesn't hold a candle to out-and-out mental disarray

With one exception: it puts an end to usual ways of speaking
    and behaving

Periodically rising above the longing
My poem to you is difficult to pin down
With one exception: it puts an end to usual ways of speaking
    and behaving
Like October entering earth's atmosphere in flames

["Song," p. 131]

TRANSLATION

The windowed construction is the rusted color of a cruller
and the insubstantial hues on the other side,
not excluding hard-edged shade,
have *kruller* written all over them.

> Knowing the correct order
> letters appear in a word
> won't make you a C.E.O.; neither
> (cf. the new "rocket ship"
> apartment buildings)
> are there regulations when it comes
> to the big shapes of the city:
> the macro-economics of personal identity

supplying motives for buying this or
that product, influencing life choices
that excite but rarely go beyond the talking stage
before they sputter and hiss and go dark

["Building Sixteens," p. 143]

TRANSLATION

In somewhat the same fashion . . . the split down the middle
Makes it highly unlikely that a new contract will prove stable

★

At the same time the dramatization of disaster races
Past its ritual beginnings and embraces (or tries

★

Rain and fog in the forecast. It feels like the bright hours are
    stumbling
From their unroofed deck towards the murk of evening

★

Important lack or want, striving for individual gain, anxiety,
    narrow-minded perceptions,
Hammered into a screen at the verge of ultimate questions

★

Instead of joining up and taking it back from ends
To ways of doing—so navigation has no margins

*

I remember seeing reproductions of Italian water pitchers
That looked like sea dragons in animated features

*

Roundabout as though a boa constrictor swallowed the past.
After keeping the water on one side and the land on the other,
    you take the last

*

Yellow flowers "as continuous as the stars that shine,"
Half-created by the perceiver. There is no direct line

*

A useful hypothesis may appear paradoxical
(Sun-showers being one parallel)

*

Spread-eagled inseparable from sudden deafening violence
Brought about by misdirection—only now your license

*

Think of the inevitability of *blue* modifying *sky*,
And that duplication can be equally pleasing to ear and eye

★

As a still life with a jar of olives may persist as a standard
Of beauty—until an artist comes along who is more wayward

★

All the mountains and streams, fields and clouds visible through
    windows
Get bigger; in turn, the issue of appearance vs. essence
    undergoes

★

Small, fleshy, red-to-purple berries obstinately linked to tears
In a basic category error. Whereas a city's decline over years

["Fourteen Poems," p. 103]

DEONTOLOGY

and the Belmonts.
All the same, you don't consider unexpressed desires
comparable to expressed ones. The sun
has no unexpressed desires save the satin ruse
that has picked up the filters and saved them, favorites
long past, things leveled

and moved to the thesis box
in semblable grace, like the stars
no one really likes, horsehair und tinder,
smudges of time's *noir*.

The pawky dream shelf is next to what's best,
talking about the binges of Nextville

but in a higher plane.

June 16. Sun then no sun then sun then no sun for the foreseeable future.

June 20. The species have the life.

June 22. Listening to the Mozart Clarinet Concerto on the radio with the a/c on and they play it all the way through. Not that an isolated movement can't be enjoyable in spite of oneself. Competent and more but not as good as it should be—he muttered, after not having played it through cleanly for years! Actually, I was pretty sure I knew who it was right from the start, tonguing if anything *too* fast, a little show-offy, even some roughness in fast passages.

Faster than the wild turkeys who clearly know where their safe havens lie and make a beeline for them regardless of who notices, their collars graven round about.

So who was it.

June 24. A tiny—though probably not as tiny as it looked from where I was sitting—brown bird hung in the air like a hummingbird then shot off while others were busy exploring below. Downwind of roses.

The pair of cardinals that zip around like flying drops of blood . . . let's make that like ice-dancers, especially when compared to the deliberate hawks. The latter have a continuous relationship but a continually shifting one, so that a straight line connecting them at any given moment is one of an infinite number of variables. Neither is what we mean by chaos, but each has a somewhat unsettling if partly pleasing randomness. A blood bank of cardinals. A plane geometry of hawks.

A throwback of oafs. An Assignment of Poems (for KK).

June 25. Rainy and esoteric.

June 26. Light rain with a thick border of drizzle.

June 29. We don't ordinarily think of clouds as minds, but they exhibit some of the same forms of detachment, from "spacing out" to "scattering" to disintegration. Plus the appearance at least of being superimposed, more convincingly at certain times than at others.

July 1. Stammering.

July 3. Stammering until after dark.

July 5. How about coming back as a *bad* poet or a *bad* painter?

The turn in English cattle-breeding (domesticated animals generally) comes in the mid-18th century with the so-called improvements—the Cardboard Bull with the piercing eye and internal organs worn on its hide; the Heartbreaking White Ram with the second "ram" clinging to its underside; legions of horses, chickens and pigs, and notably the Improved Suffolk Pig (painted in 1862 by the prolific animal portraitist John Vine as a thoughtful duffel bag) and the 802- lb. Spherical Pig, which lived to the age of 2½, a tragic football inflated for prizes (painted and later engraved after the painting), its tiny trotters far too small and glued on to hold up its colossal body.

July 6. Dark again, wet, a little screwy in the topgallants, meaning. . .not very.

This is how the schedule is shaping up:

> Uglification
> Writing off
> Gladly yearning (& gladly leaching)
> Hegemony
> Pseudopoetics
> Breast period
> Abscess
> Colonization
> Higher myth

It isn't written in stone.

July 8. King Lear walks into a bar. Why the subdivision?

July 10. Trying to get hot, trying to get cool, trying to appear nonchalant but not fumblingly as in *sprezzatura*, which is clearly over-rated—at least once you make it out of your teens, which this summer clearly has done.

July 11. Méséglise drops: "Never drifting apart, never wandering off on their own during their rapid course, but each one keeping its place and drawing its successor in its wake."

July 15 (for John Ashbery). The factory, which was a 6-floor building in the garment district, lasted for about a decade, and then only because the authorities were paid to look the other way. It wasn't all fangs and blood, but there were a lot of tie-ins. The female employees were named Velma. I worked one summer as their elevator operator, and was amazed at what you can get used to. Not that I was exactly thrilled by my wolf costume—nor did anyone appear to care much about the inevitable confusions between worker and product. There was something both exalted and exalting about the absolute stillness and high blue sky underneath which the wolves stood at strict attention, just before the whistle blew for lunch.

July 19. The same late afternoon clouds, I swear, as yesterday—

unlike the cow dung the philosopher Heraclitus lay down in, in legend and apparently also in fact, in order to cure his dropsy, only to be eaten by a pack of wild dogs who evidently found the combination too enticing to circumvent twice.

July 22. How about brown light through a rose window, there's your wine-dark sea.

—I did that already.

Socks made of wool
facing feet made of sheep.

Hogs report to shingled roof. On the double.

Make room.

July 28. Suppose the dreams are getting advices, what does "advice" mean. Suppose it means I advise you to read this and hope very much that you will be able to do so.

July 29. The rain finally came and finally left. In between, steady downpour followed by incredible, which is to say, computer-generated, fog—strands, fronds, wall hangings, tarpaulins, dark disdain—rising from below ground and threatening to foreclose on air. It thinned out a little on the open highway, only to gather elsewhere with a lumpish vengeance. The tiny white toads flopping across the winding lane by the pond seemed as terrified as the fleeing deer in *Bambi*, but for all anyone knows they could have been enjoying themselves, like a dog that gets a chance to let loose after being cooped up in an apartment all day.

Unmannerly threats, the chess champion Reuben Fine,
  adipose tissue, Dvorak's *humoresque*

July 30. A Hunt Cantata of clouds.

Aug. 1. Interesting that "petrified" means extreme fright when in reality both fight and flight involve extremes of action rather than being turned to stone. Hearts made of stone. Too long a sacrifice can make a stone of the heart. Is that, the paralysis factor, what was going on with the Medusa, shutdown of the autonomic nervous system, coma so to speak of everything in sight?

I keep staring at the space underneath a large—sycamore tree it looks like, darker than one would imagine even in bad weather. Than I would have imagined.

Well, stop.

Aug. 2. A water pipe crawled out of the woods.

Aug. 4. I am in front of a large college audience about to give my opening Charles Eliot North Lecture, but before I can utter a word someone asks a question and I spend the entire time trying to answer it. I have something written on a paper on top of the lectern, but I've never seen the paper before and the writing doesn't look like English. When the allotted time is up I get some seemingly genuine applause. The wall at my back is all glass. Behind it is a "planned miniature forest" built for the occasion, into which everyone rushes the second the applause stops.

Aug. 5. Ceci n'est pas un diary.

Aug. 6. A pretty good morning: clear, well-defined clouds; no overreaching. Towards midday less well-defined so the reach was ambiguous—ultimately prophetic as it darkened uncontrollably and began to pour and never stopped. So: an alert start, followed by a short but emblematic gray area, and a largely bitter, peaty finish.

Aug 9-13. Stammering.

Aug. 14. The *pas moi*. And what, exactly, do I mean by that.

I mean it shows.

(P.M.) Thirty or so of the neighborhood turkeys poking down the hill; rest period underneath the cedars; loud thunderclap;

246

some rain; names not as rigid but rigid enough; sun a hero but so are the simulacra, one with a yarmulke and playing Klezmer clarinet; you with the raptness emblazoned; wave function denied access so it pops up elsewhere, like Chopin in the 20th century; November till noon; oscillations of October; art and the trucks; Liszt at the Kit Kat Club.

Aug. 19.   This Netting-and-Thug capital I keep trying to write about is beginning to seem like a theme park rather than a hospital . . . though clearly the thugs have little if anything to do. Mostly they just stand around as though on an endless coffee break. Could they conceivably be taking part in some unannounced job action? Most likely they have simply ceased to function in the manner to which I am accustomed, which brings up the interesting issue of when they stop being thugs and have to be called by some other name.

On the other hand and perhaps more to the point, the netting is *too* palpable, all cords and no interstices, like a crawlspace whose floorboards are nowhere and whose low ceiling is everywhere.

Aug. 21. I heard a deer *honk* when I woke up. Quietly so as not to wake anyone else.

Aug. 24. A long line of vehicles, from 18-wheelers to mountain bikes and those silver scooters that were so popular a couple of years ago, stacked up in front of a rural railroad crossing, ridge of foothills in the distance. Two large heavyset men in dark business suits and white socks, pants a little too short, lying on their sides on the grass intent on fixing something at track level.

The postcard version of life gets an unnecessarily bad rap. It's one among many, not necessarily false or reductive. To say it distorts the *tone* of life is to describe in a realistic manner an aspect of life that is as real as any other.

Aug. 25.   Rain promised again—strange sort of promise—but zilch so far (mid-afternoon). Whole blocks of sky moving slowly as if painfully, or as if hiding something that would be painful if revealed.

Just before dusk a strip of bluish acetate like the thin wash of clouds the saints go marching in.

Aug. 29. IMPOSTERS BLAST PERPS!

Actually I'm almost positive it's impasto, and probably turps as well, as in artists' turpentine, so painting is somewhere close by if not in the apartment this second. What is here are the baboons, who have waited patiently for their *babooneries,* put their right paws in, take them out, put them in again, shake them, and spatter paint over the sidewalk, the open hydrant, the parked cars, the lamppost bases, the first-floor window panes and –guards, as well as their own colorful smocks and neatly organized palettes.

Sept. 2. Grisaille.

Sept. 4. Life being serially monogamous.

Sept. 8. Dark dark dark, then a hint of blue, then the sky which had been working hard all day to get clear finally did so. A blue-collar day, but with some elegance (Dave DeBusschere—though arguably the whole of the 1970-73 Knicks).

Sept. 12. Air sweetened by foreheads.

Sept. 13. Music from somewhere below, too far away to distinguish. For some reason the name "Morpeth Rant" came to mind—is that, as I dimly (probably inaccurately) recall, an old ballad which I used to play when I was a beginner? Could it be, though I don't know what it would mean, "Morpeth Rath"? Possibly an English town? A path across a moor? I can't imagine it's "Wrath"—unless it has something to do with a fight or battle, which is possible: Sing, goddess, of the wrath of _____. Not that rant and wrath are so different.

Sept. 14. What am I a lyre or a sink.

Late afternoon shafts of freckled gold like alto sax reeds. With a green matte varnish.

The dark is boyish when you think about it.

Sept. 17. I'm struck, as I'm sure others are, by the "shalt" in Donne's "Death thou shalt die" sonnet. A lot more than by Dylan Thomas's (hardly read any more is my guess) "And death shall have no dominion." The imperative mood attached to the future tense, i.e., wish as much as forecast. A wishful forecast. There *will be* no more dying. *Then.*

Let me know.

Sept. 18. Speaking of scattering, isn't there a rhetorical term for loosening a word from its proper object and letting it drift to something that's merely in the vicinity? Allen Ginsberg does it in "Howl" as do a lot of others. Looking for an angry fix. O moon with how sad steps thou climb'st the sky.

The line stretching between the two Hotels de Ville across Broadway was visible for a few minutes early this morning—a thin, fleeting metonymy. How come air conditioners, vacuums, major appliances, etc., aren't given seductive names like cars? The Fedders Igloo. The Friedrich Zero Tolerance. Electrolux Suck-Up.

Oxford UP has *The Philosophy of Avenues* slated for fall 2005 or spring 2006.

Sept. 20-22. Obsessive-compulsive humidity.

Sept. 25. The ghost of a day. Partly rainy. Partly sunny. Partly

250

not there.

Sept. 26. A colorful morning inside a lucite frame. The autumn of the highway thrown in for effect, but the effect is mixed: ground down like incisors, already some chipping and resurfacing, occasional uprooting followed by wholesale restoration, bridgework, new posts, etc. The day that started out as though it would be bright and pleasantly breezy, even a little chilly for September, but fell in with bad company and wound up deteriorating in just about every sense, including the spiritual, isn't a rigid designator.

Sept. 28. The following are rigid designators: Johnny Vander Meer, Johnny Friendly, Peter Unger, Marjorie Perloff, The Man That Corrupted Hadleyburg, the Widow Wadman, Ralph Waldo Emerson, Julie Schwarz, Ken Schwarz, the Sears Tower. The man who wrote *Seven Types of Ambiguity* isn't a rigid designator, as there is nothing necessary about his having written that book, or about the fact that what he did write had that name, or even that he was a critic in addition to being a poet. We can imagine possible worlds where he taught shop or raced Formula 1 automobiles. The notion of rigid designator is intuitively satisfying and "stood analytic philosophy on its ear," as one of the blurbs on the back of Saul Kripke's landmark *Naming and Necessity* attests. Yet the man who wrote *Naming and Necessity* isn't a rigid designator, nor is the man who presented the substantial text of what would become the book at Princeton in a series of three lectures (with no notes) over a period of just over a week in January 1970, which for its importance rivals (if it doesn't exceed) Allen Ginsberg's reading of "Howl" in 1955. Yet exciting as those three evenings must have been for the philosophy community and the history of ideas in general, the use of a rigid designator for something or someone who no longer exists brings with it a poignancy that can sometimes verge on the intolerable, and that amounts, at least arguably, to designating a (rigid) designator, i.e., something that formerly referred in a rigid way to the same person in all possible worlds but now refers, in a far paler way, to a cluster of qualities, appearance, life's work, etc., that exists only in or as memory. That is to say, we continue to use the designation—or pretend to use it, though with no pejoratives attaching to pretend—in the same way even though, rather than being the same reference, it is somehow cut off before it has a chance to travel very far—I would go so far as to suggest, before it has a chance to really get started—hence really more of a stammer than a reference, or else a stammered reference, the non-referential aspect becoming progressively clear as well as progressively poignant over time. Rather than having its meaning or meaningfulness in some counterfactual world, it resides wholly in this one whereas the person designated no longer does, the gap between the two being such as to be progressively intolerable. It isn't, that is to say, like either Johnny Friendly or Remedios the Beauty, but rather like Robert Campin or Jacqueline du Pré.

Sept. 30. It isn't as though the designation itself is any less rigid (there are no other candidates for the object of the designation) but that what is designated is "different from what it was before it changed," as Thomas Hardy would put it, in the possible, i.e., logical, worlds in which it formerly had its meaning. Nor is it a mental shorthand. And yet we continue to use it (or pretend to use it) in the same way, even though the reference itself is cut off almost before it has a chance to get started, so that it is really more of a stammer than a reference, a stammered reference, the non-referential aspect becoming clearer as well as increasingly poignant as time passes.

NEW POEMS

ADVICE

1

Suppose the dreams are
getting advices, what does
"advice" mean. Suppose it
means I want you to read this, and
hope very much that you are
able to do so.

2

Jason lassos Medea
and winter piles up, distinguished
by its rich inner life from
thieving sunset. Bring it
in a little? Would Scarr and
Sue please mug more directly—not *more*—
into the camera? Bulk as
waywardness, waywardness under the romance

of whatever branches it chooses,
in most of the constructions.

Everything Keeps on Happening

Which is why they laminate the newspapers
and put them up a few feet above the Callery pear trees
(the only trees that can silently read)

For example, a thick sheen like a sun with a broken yolk

But what happens is that the noumenal is invariably
the issue, throwing the switch awkwardly one way
and then rapidly the other so it's impossible to say
more than could be said if nothing in fact were happening—so
imperceptibly it feels awkward to be noticing

MIND AND BODY

1

The Catskills (Schumann) vs. the Adirondacks (Webern).

2

The periodic table shifts—shifted in its sleep.
Sends best wishes to the pond *tout court*
so scum, mud, projection, low-hanging mist and night are
    scapegoats.

3

The earth is hacked into three slabs each covered with oak
    bark and numbered.
Two-fifths of consciousness is heroic in the same way
dusk is heroic: on its own, less shamed by cosmic sprawl
than by rags of knowledge which, torn hastily,
tied together and hanging from an upper-story window,
smell of turpentine.

4

Life (that bearing wall) dedicates poem
to the giant cloud with a nose (superhero).

5

O girl singers wide awake and brighter than Alpha Centauri.
O heavy-handed moon.
A delicate white butterfly circumvents an almost
    unrecognizable spruce
still in terrible shape from the ice storm of months ago,
needing a big push back.

6

Hairline of cedars turns
into affable human being
then back into feathery tips and speaks.
The air is a drip!
Too many brains sitting around like toadstools
and noodling, when they aren't practicing scales
well into the night.

7

I like to think of still-lifes as "absent mind"
but of course every curling lemon peel is "a thought in readiness"
and the theory that this is not only the world but its best face,
the aspect that joins us most closely to what we feel,
falls headfirst into an empty white ceramic vase,
shoelaces flopping over the rim.

8

A deer, a cow, and three wild turkeys
look up from the oil painting
they are trying gamely but unsuccessfully
to step out of. Not so the sycamores with
their scaly, too open love—as to which we hope
they will soon publish their lyrics.

9

Try whistling Chopin. You try.
The shade is approximately five feet off the ground, fully alert.
Loops around a low cedar branch.
Texts its future self
before tying itself up into thick brown knots.
Forty-eight epigraphs and
a Shakespearean sonnet
couldn't keep me from you.

Enter Ghost

And what do you think of an inference that gobbles up differences
right or wrong,
or anything that smacks of interpretation.

    The restless palaver: restlessness
    plus circummuring. A bench warmer
    on the side of meaning well (despite being
    dangerously overdetermined).

Suspected that the faces inside are equal to or greater than
what you see from the vantage of your divided life.

Poem Beginning with an Early Poem

I pick up a magazine of poems
then I pick up a book of poems
then you are sitting naked under a wash of leaves.

Poetry is astounding
if you don't spend too much time on it.

As today, March 4, 1886
the air is a trio sonata for recorders and continuo.
The systematic derangement of the senses is a go.
Erections are hard. Poetry is difficult.

CLOUDY BRIGHT

1

Helplessly illuminated, as if by some new sort of lightbulb containing a poisonous gas which has been approved by the EPA.

2

By themselves the windows with their decorated spandrels are interesting enough, but they seem phoney in bulk. Everyone's thoughts aimed at everyone else, so what could conceivably pass for delicacy (of feeling as well as discrimination) is rounded off if not flattened to a pancake. Not gray or grayish white, or gray with a cream-colored wash, or gray steaming up from ordinary blacktop. Tiny brownish-gray birds like window plants from far across town.

3

She's all states
(and mooning assistants)

4

Or assailants? Probably not. Uncommonly bright for what is fundamentally dark—in a nice way; like, say, pine woods stretching far back behind a house with too many Christmas lights. The soul small as it is (hard to tell it apart from its mouthpieces, which seem articulate enough sometimes, more often along the lines of "pre-speech") splitting into its cast of thousands, subatomic doesn't begin to tell the story.

Two Tunes

1

The Bank Clerk's Tale
with the shaded windows.
It would be nice, wouldn't it, if reality so-called

imitated *us* for a change. Two golden retrievers,
watching over a 19th-century wheat field.
The cheekbones flame. Cut to long, dark brown hair.

2 (Night Walks into a Bar)

O my love
but you don't know where to put it.
The new building has it

then it doesn't have it
no one has anything!
Clouds as pots de crème.

THE FUTURE

"The future's so bright I gotta wear shades"—Timbuk 3

"The future is dark, which is on the whole, the best
thing a future can be, I think"—Virginia Woolf

TILL THEN

The possibility
that we are all volume

LATER

A museum in hot pursuit

NO ... NORD ... DU

Nothing doing! Christmas lights go on, on top.
Shredded stars—it's a lousy gazetteer.
Many books are lousy, spread-eagled
as tillers, splashed in their accumulated
flight plans

WHILE YOU WERE OUT

Foo. The long view has a talking horseshoe crab.
Evening and the perps, craning their necks. . . . Evening
is a scherzo and not a coda to anything
and gets the contract extension because—because
of the wonderful things it does

VOLUMETRICALLY

NEIGE DOLOROSA

Cut it out! All it is,
formulated and not, as the pre-existing
head thinks in any meaningful way

      I mean flush as head and heart
      in the deposition category.

The roofs are immortal, not so unstinting care
one of the things you see over a city piled high with
    representations.
The clouds recuse themselves. Please extend the sign

to include you shooting beyond the undesirable
but reasonable idea, push/pull in doing so
but no regeneration. So neige dolorosa.

268

Hommage à Ponge

1

Some of the things it is best known for: Movies rarely if ever do it justice! Although it could be said to exist without its several prostheses (which are interesting and beautiful enough in themselves to be objets d'art), once fitted together it forms "a more perfect union." Yet it isn't a god: of Prosthesis or anything else. It looks from the side as though its head is on backwards. It isn't really Janus-faced. Although it appears to be promiscuous, its promiscuity is a chaste promiscuity—and in fact one would do far better to think in terms of serial monogamy if not lifetime union.

2

The promiscuity issue is an interesting one in light of its prosthetic tongue (as well as head, neck, and elegant sling) and willingness to share bodily fluids forever and forever and forever (why should it climb the lookout). It is the furthest thing from X-rated or lubricious. If approached improperly it thwarts relentlessly. Yet if approached in a suitable way it can raise its partner and itself to unearthly heights. The risk of infection: zero.

3

Mark but this gold swan and mark how, while neither a god nor its representation, it can be worn around the neck as a jewel or amulet. Its several prostheses could be museum pieces. Nor does it make sense to talk in a meaningful way about a swan song since in theory as well as in most practice its song is endless. What appear to be silences are tacet measures.

4

As to which, apart from tacets it is nothing if not performative. It purrs and grunts (quips, barks, sings bel canto, buzzes, squeaks, whispers, yells, honks, indulges, raps, wheezes, is effortless, squeals, articulates, elaborates, exhorts, etc.). Yet it isn't a god. Mark but this swan and mark how it soars yet is down-to-earth *tout court*. It's "created half to rise, and half to fall," "crawling between earth and heaven," named: the names that are virtually parts of it: for its "isthmus of a middle state": Bird (Yardbird), Hawk, Cannonball, Fathead, Prez (President). It can be worn around the neck like an amulet or a machinist's necklace. It has pearl-like fingernails (it could be its own jewelry). Far from lubricious its moisture is a sign of life at its highest.

5

Yet movies have a terrible time doing it justice just as they have a terrible time with writers and artists in general (*The Red Shoes*, *Topsy-Turvy*, etc., being the rare exceptions that prove the rule). It's the top: it's Napoleon brandy. It has a shapely sling in addition to a prosthetic (swan's) neck, head, and gently tapering tongue. It's the close-up of an amulet or an amulet for a giant. It takes five.

270

FOR BEVERLY KENNEY

Anything fiery
or coming right out and carrying,
the spread of base blue,
the flake, insert a toothpick.

So who are you to flatten like a worldling
until the very skylarks are invited to lunch.
Man takes off jacket in effort to increase wingspan. Success!
And the wind muscles the stars around.

POETRY PROCEDURAL

The pieced together, sooty (though still silvery) chimney is holding its own. The out to lunch bricks framing it, an orangey beige under layers of grime, have little to say in the matter. Nor do the mostly vertical highlights on the cylinder, which begin in a confusion of stains (almost certainly from leaks) and become brighter and more purposeful the higher they mount. After the fourth visible segment, they appear to merge into a single vertical stripe taking up, I'd say, four-fifths of the whole, with a much thinner, somewhat darker stripe on the left and a virtual line on the right—just enough to make the roundness convincing. The last pretty much disappears several segments further up towards the light source, traditionally "a flame white disk / in silken mists / above shining trees" but here and now far beyond what anyone could perceive concerning the origins of imagery or the poetic impulse.

POEM

Sad not
invisible. The determined
urge, a rosebush
standing up to the weight of things and
handpicked if that doesn't snatch

the tragic sense, open
to smoothing out a signature style.
Apart from the suggestions to sleep
comfortably (clarinet d'amour)

volume is a distraction
as well as a mask.
Villains (those guilty
of villainy) line up.
There's no need to shove.

Some days have a soul. Others
are pasted on like labels on
Italian tomato cans, cherry red, grass green
and an unearthly blue like a football team
on a billboard. I know it's
supposed to be intimate.

ACROSS

1.Visionary, to a squirrel
2. Billy Vessels
3. Sap. Proc.
4. À la Lee Konitz

The crickets, innocent, or at least blameless
(the future springs up in a cedar grove before the day, grainy
    and promising rain, masks it)
are interference rather than context, petty disarray
disinclined to come forth—as against
the thousand natural fidgetings that take in belief
and stand it on its end as though stars were fists. Imagine
naming a pond Bocca di Leone. A recessive, gene-like feeling.

Poesium; penis-like
Ape of Agath
Haberdasher to a reindeer?
Composer batting out of order
At Swim Two Birds
Dampness, civil disobedience, a rout
Feynman HS
Duino, elegiacally
Heugueste de Mousse opus
What Henry eats?

Paris–Troy dir.
Deathbed treat
Halved landscape
Success word
Anti-Semitic poet
1913–1946

MIDNIGHT BLUE

Spring is a big bag.
The 2 a.m. air circummuring the buildings
according with strings. Some heroes,
historiography (a hay field),
goodness planted like a headstone.
That the months line up before
they turn back into WW II fighters
and simply take off,
reluctantly but purposefully.

In Fairness

After asserting its right to the rain-slick roof
(which is the apartment's halo if not
its legal counsel) the darkness of the future
as praised by Virginia Woolf is a night baseball game
transformed by stadium lights, plus an aura
of real time, the way the inevitable passers-by
are portions of the base path and
not the infield grass.

This much I know or at least think—all mysteries
have consequences that appear in time, even if
the aura never quite leaves along with the
synchronous sense (which takes a rather
dim view of cause and effect) given the fluid nature
of darkness, as well as fairness.

Pictures from Bruegel

Rodeo

Guy—really a pink shirt and the flat top of a round brown cap—brings down hog with the help of a hunting knife, then replaces knife in holster slit on hog's underside.

Two pensive monkeys chained heartbreakingly to a metal ring in a high, thick-walled window arch (no glazing) which looks out behind on a pale harbor and filmy blue and green city in the far distance. Clearly the monkeys are conscious; have consciousness. We know what it is like for them to have given up hope and to look only inward, while appearing to stare at the ring imprisoning them and the space just below the window in front, between it and us.

DEATH'S VICTORY

A laugher, as they say about certain baseball games. Hollow–
eyed (and in every other conceivable way).

Dead End Kid/Servant in warm reddish brown, sea blue, and cherry red, mindlessly sucking the last drop of something good from her right index finger, while her thumbnail glints and a crust of bread smeared with something cream-colored sits brightly in her lap like a lit bulb.

Everything is in sharp silhouette and from behind, or above: hunters, obedient dogs, poles of trees, workers, skaters, birds like fat twigs. Setting: green ice and green sea of sky into which the hunters are about to proceed with their dogs (three workers plus a child looking on are the only ones who choose to stay apart and retain at least hints of physiognomy). Everything else snow except for tiny roofs or steeples and much larger rock outcroppings (having the most in the way of feature) which project above it.

"The nothing that is"—almost; trudging, hovering, balancing,
    menacing

Forest of brown lances and green armor against background of green hills with a few hard-looking buildings on top and a tiny caravan on the move in their direction. Two red, two yellow, and two light gray-green banners above the lances are the presiding Olympian gods.

ARIA FOR DOLPHIN (BLACK & WHITE)

A trio of them, having rescued the virtuoso lyrist Arion (about to be killed by pirates who seized his prize money) face out at bottom during rightmost dolphin's solo. Confusion of lines, curves, solids (sails, masts, wave crests, clouds), spatial orientation. The "human" look on the singer in the middle suggests defiance but possibly mere intentness, whereas the soloist throws his head back open-mouthed (Jolson; the Chinese brother who swallowed the sea in the folk tale) and the one on the left, slightly disconnected, humming backup, muses ahead to the next number, a tightly harmonized melodic shriek à la the McGuire Sisters.

In a corner on the extreme right, while exceptionally important gifts are changing hands, an intelligent-looking peasant is wearing a pair of early eyeglasses, crudely but effectively fashioned of some base metal and muddy-looking glass.

DISTRACTION

A guy in waders and a red jump suit braces himself in a spotlighted (from below?) eddy in the middle of a stream, while holding a mushroom fan in one hand and gesturing wildly heavenwards with the other—taking no notice of a six-foot eel walking on the water towards him, or a person stuffed into a bottomless basket hanging from the bark-like broken roof of a decrepit shack, or a double set of bare buttocks sticking out of a ragged hole in a tiny compartment attached to a crumbling brick wall, or a saint being posed in the foreground by a photographer's assistant.

A gold swath, or path. Apart from a few at work scything and baling (wearing Walt Whitman white workshirts), a silent conversation group—eating, drinking from bowls, slicing bread, not looking at each other or in any way beyond the Self. Two faceless balers behind bend into V's like the tepee shapes of the bales already formed. Close-up: the inner life. Middle distance: uncut (except for path) wall of hay as thick as several houses. Jump cut to long shot: blue-green grass and trees; paler gold thatched roofs and flattish roll of hills; faraway water, strips and necks of flat coastal land, atmospheric mist.

FOOTNOTE (HAIBUN)
to Paula

In some if not all of Manet's wash drawings in the margins—and frequently competing for space with if not actually obliterating the handwriting—of his intimate notes to women friends from the early 1880s, it isn't clear whether the plums, peaches, apples, flowers on stems, almonds and chestnuts, women's hats as well as legs below the hem of the dress, flags, a watering can, a cat, etc., are "illuminating" the message or riding roughshod over it, in some cases making it all but unreadable. Not exactly "beauty is nothing but the beginning of terror, which we still are just able to endure" [Rilke, via Stephen Mitchell], but simply that what is beautiful is somehow privileged or else nothing is, never mind what rides roughshod or obliterates or slashes through, or in what context, as these lovely, modest watercolor and ink sketches propose.

Beauty and sorrow are both slashers. So nu. So sue me.

So Much Writing

unaffected by deciphering,
all the transfers tired of *us*,
tired of the little that

flails in deference to what belongs to no one
nor should it, given an older
brain that isn't old enough to remember being a celebrant

quarreling with newly generated forms
for current life to make use of. It makes me
think those who play it safe go unnoticed

in compensation for compensation's
sake, whether in love or the episteme's
built-in subterfuge as part of atmospheric distance

as opposed—say—to all contemplation
or all street signs, contemplative in treating
you as a breath from the river, dark plush.

You Don't Want to Live in Elsinore

Solved. The horizon
looks slept in.
More ridged than daylight on its way to Delft
whose buildings have little if any inner experience.

So hand it over. It doesn't have to
stand for looking as though all there is
takes place in no more than three hours, like the sparrows
up half the night reading their work
to anyone who will listen—definitely not the streetlights
addicted to the collective, or the small green park
still tousled after last night's steady downpour.

Sneak thief makes off with seared tuna
but leaves the roasted tomatoes. What do I
think? Like the idea of a rational ethics
there's always too much left flopping, the bird-sized world along
with the jewelry of the ribcage. The painterly portions
tug from behind. Those lost are slick
and can be anything they want including inspissated.

VOYAGE TO JAPAN

Voyage northeast the mortar pluck
Retaining each its structural

Whom thought disclosed snowed on
The robe of desire

First according to
Beauty's hazel-eyed

Therefore are we turtles
Tumbling to the middle sphere

Kicked
Released into a nothingness

Around their respective clovers
Rehearse awhile your song

Architecture comes to soften the shift
On the strength of a slight centrifugality

Winds itself
Enough fingers but no real hands

Stolid as hay
Quick-rising these Vermonts and Connecticuts

To be and be suspended
This would seem to indemnify the peaks

All contraries even adaptive
Hope's coloratura has smeared and won

Roiling the pumpkin field
And the thousand water lights of Japan

ELEGIACAL STUDY

while nothing wraps the heart in newsprint

or represents its transposition
to the kitchen table.

★

Like certain coins in certain raids
few cornerstones face their saints—in the case
of the awning sung about half the evening
under strenuous lighting.

MAY

5/2

Lovely two hours, though the sky is too bright to take in, something wrong with the spot.

Awkwardness and beauty in concert aren't heroic any more than turpentine is, or spruce branches that stick out from the mass like capital letters. A brown one and a buzzing one.

5/11

The day of the mourning doves.

Solid-looking white clouds moving in tandem towards the east so slowly they could be night—Juliet being the sun—and if each blank (phrase, verse, halo, cleat mark) is a former clump, then time's wedge is a vase of peonies shot through with sunlight.

5/13

Dear Tragicomic Captains of Industry, the prickly oaks in their allover heraldry

> *can it.* It's so
> still you can hear
> a contact lens drop. A
> sliver of pinkish charcoal

now it's gone along with
the framing devices

that went out with intentionality. So the senses are inexact *and* constitutive. Which doesn't put an end to positive thinking. Or the nouveau braininess.

AFTER YEATS

1

The ground opens up. Which means that in reality it closes a part of a large space previously unnoticed. Flecked with white like a sky in February, or an Oxford shirt.

2

The ginkgo leaves are part air, part cheesecloth, like the softeners between lens and faces in old movies. This one has a few full-fledged gaps through which all the poetry gets "lost in translation." It isn't escapist to want to live forever, and to remember what to ask for—not necessarily eternal youth, rather something like eternal absence of old age, chronic illness, plagues, etc. Enter and exit ghost.

3

In the pre-war buildings that run together like streams, the urgency travels in what I would call a human way. It's hard to tell the height of one roof from the cutting edge of another. Elevated, though not extravagantly, like her forehead over her eyes.

CAFFÈ DELLE MUSE
  for Tony Towle

1

Rimbaud solves the Saturday *Times* Crossword in four minutes
and Mallarmé puts all his students to sleep—in a thoughtful
    way, like
a cat stepping agilely over a pile of sheet music.

2

An eight-foot pooka, resplendent in gray fedora and matching
    striped tie,
licks the crema from his espresso and writes the framing sentence
for a short story to be set in 1930s Dublin.

3

What do you say to a cappuccino with a poem floating on top
—which when all is said and done is an allegory of hope,
    certainly a case could be made.
Take the leaves you can still just about glimpse in fraught
    Washington Square Park
whose ongoing construction is threatening to send NYU students
up to Columbia, or down to Battery Park; not that they
would necessarily mind and, granted, not much; as Lewis
    Carroll would say,
a Liddell goes a long way.

4

Speaking of which, October is the sellers' market
whereas July, June and parts of September merely breathe out,
warm as sun brushing a window plant.

The street with a thug at either end has buildings in the
    Federal style,
the flat fronts gaining in immediacy what they sacrifice of life
    in the round,
like the wet cartoon (Firenze) or the notion that there is a
    single green vegetable superior to all others.

5

I like the image of Hart Crane bursting from a back room
with a red face and a poem hot off the typewriter.
O crooner of the forms of restlessness, the presumption of
    reason
has us all in its spell but says as much about presumption as
    about anything else!
They were waspish. They ate, drank and constructed
their surprisingly durable dwellings in the manner of wasps.
Manhattan rises from its stone bench to object,
then sits back down as the sun reaches its goal, a mica stone set
    in a mica sea.

Seasons of the Poem

    1

The creeps creep in from day to day—exit
when you're finished.
Consciousness was the *plant*
(underscoring the suspicion
that we were never meant to have it)
and the face of winter over the George Washington Bridge,
which could also have been a plant,
misrepresents its recent past,
flowing then merely ongoing.

How much does presence stand to gain?

    2

William Carlos Williams
Pablo Neruda
John Keats
Wallace Stevens (and Emily Dickinson)

I'm going to tell you how your seasons got misplaced.
                              No I'm not.

Even a quick look reveals the difference
between what the Germans used to call *schmutzmaler,*

bad painter, and the real thing; like
"vagrant" and "migrant," migrant conveying
a sense of purpose however uncertain
of outcome, an impalpable mass,
flake white, soft pedal on an upright.

A DRAGON-FREE ENVIRONMENT

Along with breathing's
disregard, I'd say
for nuances.

By the time the suspension bridge
reaches the other side, time is
the extreme case if not upwards
of pure space—ya mug, whaddaya

say to a cat-fur beer along
with the questions that fly across the switchboard?
Specially wide and colorful

paths they wear out
by the light of the moon.

CLOSE-UP

At long last, which would be
called exile if
not for a charmed life shimmering, specifically
the light that bolted

plus a red face to go with it
bigger than life. From that point on
an administrator to some, partial to new developments
in an unfriendly world. But you get rid of the underworld.

Charles North was born in 1941 in Brooklyn and has lived most of his life in and near New York City. In addition to his books of poetry, which include *The Year of the Olive Oil*, *The Nearness of the Way You Look Tonight*, *Cadenza*, and *Complete Lineups*, he has published a collection of essays on artists, critics and poets, *No Other Way*, and collaborations with artists and other poets. Since 1997 he has been Poet-in-Residence at Pace University NYC. More information available at charlesnorth.net.